Highlighted in Yellow

Highlighted in Yellow

A short course in living wisely and choosing well.

H. Jackson Brown, Jr.

and

Rochelle Pennington

Rutledge Hill Press®

Nashville, Tennessee

A Division of Thomas Nelson, Inc.

Published by Rutledge Hill Press, a division of Thomas Nelson, Inc., P.O. Box 141000, Nashville, Tennessee 37214.

www.ThomasNelson.com

Pages 230–231 constitute an extension of this copyright page.

Design by Harriette Bateman.

Library of Congress Cataloging-in-Publication Data

Brown, H. Jackson, 1940–
Highlighted in yellow : a short course in living wisely and choosing well / H. Jackson Brown, Jr. and Rochelle Pennington.
p. cm.
ISBN 1-55853-834-8 (pbk.)
1. Conduct of life. I. Pennington, Rochelle, 1963– II. Title.
BJ1581.2 .B715 2001
170'.44—dc21

2001001193

Printed in the United States of America

2 3 4 5 6—06 05 04 03 02 01

www.instructionbook.com

Contents

Introduction vii

Kindness 1

Generosity 39

Simple Pleasures 75

Attitude 113

Marriage 145

Parenting 191

Acknowledgments 230

Introduction

An eight-year-old was asked about his study habits. "Well," he said, "there's stuff and there's important stuff. I try to remember just the important stuff." That worked well for him, and, you know what? It will work for us, too.

Whether you're in high school or college, or a student of life itself, the textbooks are thick and the reading list long. So many words, so little time; what's a person to do?

Get a yellow highlighter.

You can't learn it all; no one can. But you can get a pretty good feel for any material just by highlighting the main thoughts. What is it you want to remember? What do you think will be on the test? Highlight it now for easy review later.

Highlighted in Yellow is a collection of stories and quotes on some of life's dearest subjects: the importance of acting with kindness and generosity toward others, securing meaningful relationships with those we love, choosing attitudes to carry us through the common hours of everyday life, and discovering the satisfaction that comes from the appreciation and enjoyment of simple pleasures.

These are calming words, healing words, encouraging words that inspire change and reward effort. We hope they will help you live wisely and choose well.

So do the required reading. Finish your homework. Class is always in session and we're tested every day.

Kindness

The Radio Quiz

Kindness. I came to fully understand its impact in only a few short minutes while taking one of the more important examinations of my life.

The test was oral. The test giver was a radio announcer. The classroom was my car.

While traveling along in the rain on a Monday morning, a voice coming from the little speaker next to my steering wheel asked, "Can you name the last Nobel Peace Prize winner?" I knew I should remember, but the name escaped me. While I was trying to think, more questions were asked: "Can you name a recent Pulitzer Prize winner?" Again, I couldn't. "Can you name athletes who received gold medals in the last Olympics? Or the last woman to be crowned Miss America?"

Or . . . or . . . or. No . . . no . . . no. Music, literature, art, government officials, scientists—I was zero for zero and wondering how many other listeners were answering correctly.

And then it happened. A question was asked that I could answer: "Can you name the last person who told you they loved you?" My heart melted as I remembered, vividly and without hesitation, my children running for the bus that morning, yelling over their shoulders simultaneously, "Love you!"

Another question, and again I had the answer. "Can you name the last person who hugged you?" Certainly. Most definitely.

Still others: "Can you name a person who showed you kindness recently?" Of course. "Can you name a person to whom *you* showed a kindness recently?" Again, of course. Yes, of course. "Can you name someone whose smile makes a difference in your day? Or a teacher whose dedication made a difference in your life?" Yes, yes, I know. Oh, who to choose? There are so many.

The announcer spoke of the friends, neighbors, co-workers, and even strangers who touch our lives, and I continued to smile. He spoke of helpfulness, of generosity, of thoughtfulness and charity. I felt like laughing out loud. What a way to start one's day! And on a Monday. In the rain.

Kindness matters. It is longed for and lived for. The mighty accomplishments and praiseworthy achievements of the past may be chiseled in stone, but it is the quiet and lovely acts of kindness that are written on our hearts.

1 ◆ Treat everyone you meet like you want to be treated.

We have committed the Golden Rule to memory. Now let us commit it to life.

—Edwin Markham

2 ◆ Make it a habit to do nice things for people who'll never find out.

That best portion of a good man's life, his little, nameless, unremembered acts of kindness and of love.

—William Wordsworth

3 ◆ Feed a stranger's expired parking meter.

Do not wait for extraordinary circumstances to do good; try using ordinary situations.

—JEAN PAUL RICHTER

4 ◆ When someone you know is down and out, mail them a twenty-dollar bill anonymously.

Kindness is the inability to remain at ease in the presence of another person who is ill at ease, the inability to remain comfortable in the presence of another who is uncomfortable, the inability to have peace of mind when one's neighbor is troubled.

—RABBI SAMUEL H. HOLDENSON

5 ◆ Be kinder than necessary.

Three things in human life are important: The first is to be kind. The second is to be kind. And the third is to be kind.

—HENRY JAMES

6 ◆ Carry a couple of inexpensive umbrellas in your car that you can give to people caught in the rain.

Great opportunities to help others seldom come, but small ones surround us every day.

—SALLY KOCH

7 ◆ Be open and accessible. The next person you meet could become your best friend.

Behave toward everyone as if receiving a great guest.

—CONFUCIUS

8 ◆ Never underestimate the power of a kind word or deed.

It takes so little to make people happy—just a touch, if we know how to give it, just a word fitly spoken, or a slight readjustment of some bolt or pin or bearing in the delicate machinery of a human soul.

—FRANK CRANE

I expect to pass through this world but once. Therefore, if there be any good that I can do or any kindness that I can show to any fellow creature, let me do it now, for I shall not pass this way again.

—WILLIAM PENN

9 ◆ **Seek out the good in people.**

I will speak ill of no man, and speak all the good I know of everybody.

—Benjamin Franklin

10 ◆ **When you pass a family riding in a big U-Haul truck, give them the "thumbs-up" sign. They need all the encouragement they can get.**

Giving is so often thought of in terms of the gifts we give, but our greatest giving is of our time, and kindness, and even comfort for those who need it. We look on these little things as unimportant—until we need them.

—Joyce Hifler

The Circle of a Good Deed Returns

It happened decades ago in Scotland. "Help me! Help me! Someone please help me!" came the screams from a nearby bog. A poor Scottish farmer heard those cries and ran into the dangerous area to aid. There he found a boy sinking in thick, black muck. It was nearly too late for the child to be rescued, but with the farmer's help, the boy was saved.

A knock was heard at the farmer's cottage the next day. Opening the door, the peasant was greeted by a wealthy gentleman—perhaps royalty—who arrived in a stately carriage. The poor man was confused why someone of such obvious stature had come to call upon him. His question would soon be answered.

"You saved my son yesterday, and I am here to give you a reward," spoke the fine gentleman. The farmer, however, could not accept any of the money offered to him. The rich gentleman, desperately wanting to bestow a gift of gratitude on the man for his heroic deed, looked into the humble abode and spotted a young boy. "Since you helped my son, I will help yours," said the gentleman. "If you will allow me to take your child with me, I will see that he receives the finest education available in all of the country." The poor man smiled and accepted the offer.

The generous promise was kept, and the Scotsman's son later graduated from St. Mary's Hospital Medical School in London. Because of the educational gift he had received from the wealthy gentleman, the poor farmer's son, in turn, gave a gift to the world: he discovered penicillin. His name was Sir Alexander Fleming.

The nobleman's son's life would be threatened for a second time. Now grown, he lay dying of pneumonia. Ironically, it was the poor farmer's son who saved him this time when penicillin was prescribed. The nobleman, Lord Randolph Churchill, had provided for the education of Sir Alexander Fleming, and that education had saved his son, Winston Churchill.

11 ◆ Whenever you hear an ambulance siren, say a prayer for the person inside.

More things are wrought by prayer than this world dreams of.

—Alfred, Lord Tennyson

12 ◆ Never allow a friend to grieve alone.

Friendship improves happiness and abates misery by doubling our joy and dividing our grief.

—Joseph Addison

13 ◆ Be there when people need you.

If someone comes to you asking for help, do not say in refusal, "Trust in God; He will help." Rather, act as if there were no God and no one to help except you.

—Zaddik

14 ◆ Practice empathy. Try to see things from other people's point of view.

Be kind—everyone you meet is fighting a hard battle.

—Plato

15 ◆ Remember that the nicest thing you can do for yourself is to do something nice for someone else.

If you were to go around asking people what would make them happier, you'd get answers like "a new car," "a bigger house," "a raise in pay," or "winning the lottery." Probably not one in a hundred would say "a chance to help people," and yet that is what brings about the most happiness of all.

—GEORGE BURNS

16 ◆ Call three friends on Thanksgiving and tell them how thankful you are for their friendship.

Hold a true friend with both hands.

—NIGERIAN PROVERB

Is There a Santa Claus?

6:00 P.M., *December 23, 1961.* I am writing this en route from New York to Los Angeles by plane. When I get home to Honolulu tomorrow, I must have a Christmas story ready to tell to the neighborhood children. They have asked me to title it, "Is There a Santa Claus?" How can I possibly give an honest answer to skeptical youngsters?

I hope we get to Los Angeles on time. Almost everyone aboard has a connection to make.

8:10 P.M. The pilot has just given us bad news. Los Angeles is fogged in; no aircraft can land. We have to detour to Ontario, California, an emergency field not far from Los Angeles.

3:12 A.M., *December 24.* With one problem and another, we have just landed in Ontario—six hours behind schedule. Everyone is cold, exhausted, hungry, and irritable. All of us have missed our connections. Many will not make it home by Christmas Eve. I am in no mood to make up a story about Santa Claus.

7:15 A.M. I am writing this at the Los

Angeles airport. A lot has happened in the last four hours. The airfield at Ontario was bedlam. Scores of Los Angeles-bound planes had to land there. The frantic passengers—over 1,000 of them—had hoped to get word to their families that they would be late. But the telegraph office was closed, and there were endless lines at the telephone booths. No food. No coffee.

The employees at the small terminal were just as frenzied and fatigued as the passengers. Everything went wrong. Baggage was heaped helter-skelter, regardless of destination. No one seemed to know which buses would go where, or at what time. Babies were crying; women were screaming questions; men were grumbling and being sarcastic. The mob pushed and jostled, like a swarm of frightened ants, in the effort to find luggage. It hardly seemed possible that this was the day before Christmas.

Suddenly, amid the nervous commotion, I heard a confident, unhurried voice. It stood out like a great church bell—clear, calm and filled with love.

"Now don't you worry, ma'am," the voice said. "We're going to find your luggage and get you to La Jolla in time. Everything's going to be just fine." This was the first kind, constructive statement I had heard in a long while.

I turned and saw a man who might have

stepped right out of *The Night Before Christmas.* He was short and stout, with a florid, merry face. On his head was some sort of official cap, the kind that sightseeing guides wear. Tumbling out beneath were cascades of curly white hair. He wore hunting boots, as if, perhaps, he had just arrived after a snowy trip behind a team of reindeer. Pulled snugly over his barrel chest and fat tummy was a red sweatshirt.

The man stood next to a homemade push-cart, composed of an enormous packing box resting on four bicycle wheels. It contained urns of steaming coffee and piles of miscellaneous cardboard cartons.

"Here you are, ma'am," said the unusual man with the cheerful voice. "Have some hot coffee while we look for your luggage."

Pushing the cart before him, pausing only long enough to hand coffee to others, or to say a cheerful "Merry Christmas to you, brother!" or to promise that he would be back to help, he searched among the sprawling piles of luggage. Finally, he found the woman's possessions. Placing them on the push-cart, he said to her, "You just follow me. We'll put you on the bus to La Jolla."

After getting her settled, Kris Kringle (that's what I had started calling him) returned to the terminal. I found myself tagging along and helping him with the coffee. I knew that any bus wouldn't leave for about an hour.

Kris Kringle cut a swath of light through the dismal field. There was something about him that made everyone smile. Dispensing coffee, blowing a child's nose, laughing, singing snatches of Christmas songs, he calmed panicky passengers and sped them on their way.

When a woman fainted, it was Kris Kringle who pushed through the helpless group around her. From one of his cartons, he produced smelling salts and a blanket. When the woman was conscious again, he asked three men to carry her to a comfortable settee and told them to use the loudspeaker system to find a doctor.

Who is this funny little man who gets things done, I wondered. I asked him, "What company do you work for?"

"Sonny," he said to me, "see that kid over there in the blue coat? She's lost. Give her this candy bar, and tell her to stay right where she is. If she wanders around, her mother won't ever find her."

I did as ordered, then repeated, "What company do you work for?"

"Shucks, I'm not working for anyone. I'm just having fun. Every December I spend my two weeks' vacation helping travelers. It's my Christmas present to myself.

"What with this rush season, there are always thousands who need a hand. Hey, look what we have over here."

He had spotted a tearful young mother with a baby. Winking at me, Kris Kringle perked his cap at a jaunty angle and rolled his cart over to them. The woman was sitting on her suitcase, clutching her baby.

"Well, well, sister," he said, "that's a mighty pretty baby you have. What's the trouble?"

Between sobs, the young woman told him that she hadn't seen her husband for over a year. She was to meet him at the hotel in San Diego. He wouldn't know what had delayed her and would worry, and the baby was hungry.

From the pushcart, Kris Kringle produced a bottle of warmed milk. "Now don't you worry. Everything will be all right," he said.

As he guided her to the bus for Los Angeles—the one I was to leave on—he wrote down her name and the name of the hotel in San Diego. He promised her that he would get a message to her husband.

"God bless you," she said, climbing aboard and cradling the now sleeping child in her arms. "I hope you have a merry Christmas and receive many wonderful presents."

"Thank you, sister," he said, tipping his cap. "I've already received the greatest gift of all, and you gave it to me. Ho, ho," he went on, seeing something of interest in the crowd, "there's an old fellow in trouble. Good-bye, sister. I'm going over there to give myself another present."

He got off the bus. I got off, too, since the bus wouldn't leave for a few minutes. He turned to me. "Say," he said, "aren't you taking the jalopy to Los Angeles?"

"Yes."

"Okay, you've been a good assistant. Now I want to give you a Christmas present. You sit next to the lady and look after her and the baby. When you get to Los Angeles"—he fished out a piece of paper—"telephone her husband at this hotel in San Diego. Tell him about his family's delay."

He knew what my answer would be because he left without even waiting for a reply. I sat down next to the young mother and took the baby from her. Looking out the window, I saw Kris Kringle in his bulging red sweatshirt disappearing into the crowd.

The bus started. I felt good. I began thinking of home and Christmas. And I knew then how I would answer the question of the children in my neighborhood: "Is there a Santa Claus?"

I had met him.

—WILLIAM J. LEDERER

A pessimist, they say, sees a glass of water as being half-empty; an optimist sees the same glass as half-full. But a giving person sees a glass of water and starts looking for someone who might be thirsty.

—G. DONALD GALE

17 ◆ Rekindle old friendships.

Go oft to the house of a friend, for weeds choke up the unused path.

—Ralph Waldo Emerson

18 ◆ Remember that the people on our planet are not standing in a line single file. Look closely. Everyone is really standing in a circle, holding hands. Whatever you give to the person standing next to you, it eventually comes back to you.

There is a destiny that makes us brothers;
None goes his way alone.
All that we send into the lives of others
Comes back into our own.

—Edwin Markham

19 ◆ When you see someone sitting alone on a bench, make it a point to speak to them.

When you carry out acts of kindness you get a wonderful feeling inside. It is as though something inside your body responds and says, "Yes, this is how I ought to feel."

—RABBI HAROLD KUSHNER

20 ◆ Let people pull in front of you when you're stopped in traffic.

No act of kindness, no matter how small, is ever wasted.

—AESOP

You cannot do a kindness too soon, for you never know how soon it will be too late.

—Ralph Waldo Emerson

21 ◆ When you've learned that a good friend is ill, don't ask him about it. Let him tell you first.

The first duty of love is to listen.

—Paul Tillich

22 ◆ Call a nursing home or retirement center and ask for a list of the residents who seldom get mail or visitors. Send them a card several times a year. Sign it, "Someone who thinks you are very special."

Alone and without love we die. Life itself is as dependent on relationships with others as it is on food.

—M. N. Beck

A Random Act of Kindness

Every hotel in Philadelphia was full. There was not a room to be rented anywhere. The young clerk working the desk of the Bellvue Hotel on this rainy night in 1891 knew this. So when an elderly couple walked in from out of the storm in the middle of the night and approached the counter, the young man, moved with compassion, offered them the only bed available: his own. The couple refused; the clerk insisted. Through the kindly persuasion of the young man, the elderly couple finally accepted his offer.

When checking out the following morning, the couple reiterated their gratitude to the young man for the extraordinary thoughtfulness he had shown to them. “You are the kind of person who should be the manager of the best hotel in the United States,” said the gentleman. “Maybe someday I will build one for you.” The three chuckled over the man’s comment as they parted company.

The incident was forgotten by the clerk, but not by the old man. Two years later, an enormous, castle-like structure was erected in New York City by the elderly man who had been touched by the kind-hearted clerk in Philadelphia. It was now time to invite the young fellow to see the grand hotel awaiting him.

Upon his arrival, the old man took the clerk downtown. “That,” said the gentleman, “is the hotel I built for you to manage.” While standing on the street corner beside the soon-to-be world-renowned Waldorf-Astoria Hotel, the young clerk, George C. Boldt, was titled its first manager.

For the next twenty-three years, until his death in 1916, Boldt remained faithful to the hotel and to the confidence William Waldorf Astor had placed in him.

23 ◆ Wave to crosswalk patrol mothers.

It is by little acts of watchful kindness recurring daily and hourly, by words, tones, gestures, looks, that affection is won and preserved.

—George A. Sala

24 ◆ Look for opportunities to make people feel important.

There is more hunger for love and appreciation in this world than for bread.

—Mother Teresa

The Sufis advise us to speak only after our words have managed to pass through three gates. At the first gate, we must ask ourselves, "Are these words true?" If so, we let them pass on; if not, back they go. At the second gate, we must ask ourselves, "Are these words necessary?" If so, we let them pass on; if not, back they go. At the last gate, we must ask, "Are they kind?"

—Eknath Easwaran

25 ◆ When going through the checkout line, always ask the cashier how she's doing.

Nothing is ever lost by courtesy. It is the cheapest of pleasures, costs nothing, and conveys much. It pleases him who gives and him who receives and thus, like mercy, is twice blessed.

—Erastus Wiman

26 ◆ If you know someone is on a diet, tell them they're looking terrific.

A kind heart is a fountain of gladness, making everything in its vicinity freshen into smiles.

—Washington Irving

27 ◆ When you receive a kindness, pass it on.

After Benjamin Franklin had received a letter thanking him for having done a kindness, he replied: "As to the kindness you mention, I wish I could have been of more service to you than I have been, but if I had, the only thank you that I should desire is that you would always be ready to serve any other person that may be in need of your assistance in any way; and so let good deeds go around, for mankind are all a family. As for my part, when I am employed in serving others, I do not look upon myself as conferring favors but as paying debts."

28 ◆ Be the first to say, "Hello."

The opportunity for brotherhood presents itself every time you meet a human being.

—Jane Wyman

New York City, 1925: The treasurer of a Jewish hospital fund with $15,000 in his pocket was stopped by two robbers. When told the money was for a hospital, the robbers not only let the man go on his way, they threw in a ten-dollar bill of their own.

—Pitirim Sorokin

29 ◆ Smile a lot. It costs nothing and is beyond price.

They might not need me, but they might;
I'll let my head be just in sight.
A smile as small as mine might be
Precisely their necessity.

—EMILY DICKINSON

30 ◆ Cut out complimentary newspaper articles about people you know and mail the article to them with notes of congratulations.

Even the smallest act of kindness says "I care," says "You matter," says "I thought of you."

—JENNY DEVRIES

Do all the good you can,
By all the means you can,
In all the ways you can,
In all the places you can,
At all the times you can,
To all the people you can,
As long as ever you can.

—John Wesley

31 ◆ Treat others like you would want them to treat your children.

What do we live for if it is not to make life less difficult for each other?

—George Eliot

32 ◆ Make someone's day by paying the toll for the person in the car behind you.

How beautiful a day when a kindness touches it.

—George Elliston

33 ◆ Be especially courteous and patient with older people.

Resolve to be tender with the young, compassionate with the aged, sympathetic with the striving, tolerant with the weak, and forgiving with the wrong. Sometime in your life, you will have been all of these.

—Lloyd Shearer

34 ◆ Say "please" and "thank you" a lot.

Never underestimate the power of simple courtesy. Your courtesy may not be returned or remembered, but discourtesy will.

—Princess Jackson Smith

Homework

Showing kindness is an essential ingredient in a life well lived. Kindnesses need not be big; more often they are little things, spontaneous acts done on the spur of the moment. Your assignment today is to find opportunities to show a little kindness to those around you. Where do you start? Try some of these:

- Overtip a breakfast waitress.
- Compliment three people today.
- Surprise a loved one with a little inexpensive gift.
- Invite the person in line behind you to go ahead of you.
- When you see visitors taking pictures of each other, offer to take a picture of them together.
- Surprise a new neighbor with one of your favorite homemade dishes—and include the recipe.

Generosity

A Snowy Christmas Eve

I can still see him all these years later. It was Christmas Eve, 1970-something. Our high school youth program was participating in the Salvation Army fund drive as an outreach project. I stood outside a Wisconsin K-Mart, ringing a bell on the last shift of the season.

With closing time nearing, the throngs of shoppers had dwindled. The end couldn't come soon enough for me. I was freezing.

It was then that I heard the old clunker car pull into the parking lot, its windshield wipers slapping at the snow.

In a smug tone, I muttered under my breath, "It's the end of the day and this fellow still wants to come shopping?" My spirit of volunteerism suddenly blew away with the wind.

An old man got out of the car and shuffled toward me.

"Buying one last gift?" I asked, greeting him.

He seemed to consider my words. "Yes, one last gift," he softly replied.

He approached the familiar red kettle. A very large hand, gnarled like tree roots, emerged from the warmth of his coat pocket, holding four coins. Pennies? No. What then?

Tipping his hand ever so slightly, the unidentified coins fell into the belly of the kettle.

"Merry Christmas," I acknowledged. "Thank you for helping."

His very blue eyes looked up and met mine. Nodding, he responded, "I couldn't not." Then he turned and left. Just like that.

I watched him, tracks trailing in the snow, and thought to myself, *That was strange. Really strange. An old guy comes out in bad weather, on bad roads, to give a few cents to charity?*

Well, his "few cents" turned out to be a few thousand dollars. A jubilant money-counter back at headquarters recognized the coins. Krugerrands. South African in origin. Pure gold.

All these years later, the old man's words still ring with life within my memory: "I couldn't not."

His words have become, for me, a summary of the essence of generosity—the stirring within the human heart that compels one to help others for no reason other than the goodness of participating in a cause larger than oneself. These are the moments when our souls shine bright and beautiful and connect with the heart of God.

I know, for I have seen this shining in the blue eyes of an old man as he stood in the snow one Christmas Eve.

1 ◆ Choose a charity in your community and support it generously with your time and money.

On the street I saw a small girl shivering in a thin dress, with little hope of a decent meal. I became angry and said to God, "Why do You permit this? Why don't You do something about it?" And God replied, "I certainly *did* do something about it. I made you."

—Sister Mary Rose McGready

2 ◆ Take a few hours every month to deliver Meals on Wheels.

Maturity begins to grow when you can sense your concern for others outweighing your concern for yourself.

—John MacNoughton

3 ◆ Bless every day with a generous act.

Make a rule and pray to God to help you keep it, never, if possible, to lie down at night without being able to say, "I have made one human being a little wiser, or a little happier, or at least a little better this day."

—CHARLES KINGSLEY

4 ◆ Donate food for natural disaster victims.

Whenever tragedy or disaster has struck in any corner of the world, the American people have promptly and generously extended hands of mercy and help. Generosity has never impoverished the giver; it has enriched the lives of those who have practiced it.

—DWIGHT D. EISENHOWER

5 ◆ Contribute something to each Salvation Army kettle you pass during the holidays.

We should give as we would receive, cheerfully, quickly, and without hesitation; for there is no grace in a benefit that sticks to the fingers.

—SENECA

6 ◆ Remember that the benefits of a life lived with enthusiasm and gratitude are always available to you.

A man there was,
And they called him mad;
The more he gave,
The more he had.

—JOHN BUNYAN

7 ◆ Sign and carry your organ donor card.

We must not only give what we have; we must also give what we are.

—Désiré-Joseph Mercier

8 ◆ Volunteer to work a few hours each month in a soup kitchen.

What does Love look like?
It has hands to help others.
It has feet to hasten to the poor
and needy.
It has eyes to see misery and want.
It has ears to hear the sighs and sorrows
of fellow men.
That is what Love looks like.

—St. Augustine

9 ◆ Donate two pints of blood every year.

Sometimes when I consider what tremendous consequences come from little things, I am tempted to think there are no little things.

—Bruce Barton

10 ◆ Give to charity all the clothes you haven't worn during the past three years.

If you have no charity, you have the worst kind of heart trouble.

—Bob Hope

11 ◆ Get involved at your child's school.

After the verb "To Love" . . . "To Help" is the most beautiful verb in the world.

—BERTHA VON SUTTNER

12 ◆ Share your knowledge; it's a way to achieve immortality.

If something comes to life in others because of you, then you have made an approach toward immortality.

—NORMAN COUSINS

The 57¢ Difference

Many years ago in Philadelphia, a little girl named Hattie made a difference in the lives of people in her community.

A local minister started a Sunday school program for the neighborhood children, and Hattie came to the first meeting. Because the room was small, several children had to be turned away. Hattie went to bed sad that night because many of her playmates could not attend Sunday school. There just was not enough room.

Two years later, Hattie died. Her parents sent for the minister and gave him a worn red pocketbook they found beneath Hattie's pillow. The pocketbook contained fifty-seven pennies she had earned by running errands. With the money was a note in Hattie's handwriting that read, "This is to build the church bigger so more children can go to Sunday school."

The Sunday following Hattie's funeral, the minister carried the little red pocketbook into the pulpit, took out the fifty-seven pennies and dropped them one by one back into the purse.

He told how Hattie had given all she had, and the congregation was touched.

After the service, a visitor came forward and offered a piece of desirable land for a new church building. He said, "I will let the church have it for the price of *fifty-seven pennies*." When the story hit the news, checks began coming in from everywhere.

Today, visitors are impressed with the Temple Baptist Church in Philadelphia. Seating capacity for the church now is 3,300. And it all began with a little girl who wanted to help. What a difference she made!

—As cited in *From My Heart*

13 ◆ Support family members financially and emotionally when they are down.

Very few burdens are heavy if everyone lifts.

—Sy Wise

14 ◆ The next time you order takeout at a fast-food restaurant, tip the carry-out window person. He or she will be surprised and delighted.

How far that little candle throws his beams! So shines a good deed in a naughty world.

—Shakespeare

Life's most persistent and urgent question is: What are you doing for others?

—MARTIN LUTHER KING, JR.

15 ◆ Teach a Sunday school class.

A teacher affects eternity; he can never tell where his influence stops.

—HENRY ADAMS

16 ◆ Buy raffle tickets, candy bars, and baked goods from students who are raising money for school projects.

Help a child and you help humanity.

—PHILLIPS BROOKS

No Greater Love

Whatever their planned target, the mortar rounds landed in an orphanage run by a missionary group in the small Vietnamese village. The missionaries and one or two children were killed outright, and several more children were wounded, including one young girl, about eight years old.

People from the village requested medical help from a neighboring town that had radio contact with the American forces. Finally an American Navy doctor and nurse arrived in a jeep. They established that the girl was the most critically injured. Without quick action, she would die of shock and loss of blood.

A transfusion was imperative, and a donor with a matching blood type was required. A quick test showed that neither American had the correct type, but several of the uninjured orphans did.

The doctor spoke a little Vietnamese, and the nurse a little French. Using that combination, together with much sign language, they tried to explain to their young, frightened audience that unless they could replace some of the girl's lost blood, she would certainly die. Then they asked if anyone would be willing to give blood to help.

Their request was met with wide-eyed silence. After several long moments, a small hand slowly and waveringly went up, dropped back down, and then went up again.

"Oh, thank you," the nurse said in French. "What is your name?"

"Heng," came the reply.

Heng was quickly laid on a pallet, his arm swabbed with alcohol, and a needle inserted in his vein. Through this ordeal Heng lay stiff and silent.

After a moment though, he let out a shuddering sob, quickly covering his face with his free hand.

"Is it hurting, Heng?" the doctor asked. Heng shook his head no, but after a few moments another sob escaped, and once more he tried to cover up his crying. Again the doctor asked him if the needle hurt, and again Heng shook his head no.

The medical team was concerned. Something was obviously very wrong. At this point, a Vietnamese nurse arrived to help. Seeing the little one's distress, she spoke to him rapidly in Vietnamese, listened to his reply and answered him in a soothing voice.

After a moment, the patient stopped crying

and looked questioningly at the Vietnamese nurse. When she nodded, a look of relief spread over his face.

Glancing up, the nurse said quietly to the Americans, "He thought he was dying. He misunderstood you. He thought you had asked him to give *all* his blood so the little girl could live."

"But why would he be willing to do that?" asked the Navy nurse.

The Vietnamese nurse repeated the question to the little boy, who answered simply, "Because she is my friend."

Greater love has no man than this, that he lay down his life for a friend.

—John W. Mansur

17 ◆ This year, buy an extra box of Girl Scout cookies.

Nice, how we never get dizzy from doing good turns.

—George Bengis

18 ◆ Don't forget that we are ultimately judged by what we give, not by what we get.

It is more blessed to give than to receive.

—Acts 20:35

Do not care overly much for wealth or power or fame, or one day you will meet someone who cares for none of these things, and you will realize how poor you have become.

—Rudyard Kipling

19 ◆ Pay for a poor child to go to summer camp.

You have not lived a perfect day, even though you have earned your money, unless you have done something for someone who will never be able to repay you.

—RUTH SMELTZER

20 ◆ Never resist a generous impulse.

"I must do something" will always solve more problems than "Something must be done."

—FROM *BITS & PIECES*

21 ◆ Remember that the happiest people are not those getting more, but those giving more.

Joy comes not to him who seeks it for himself, but to him who seeks it for other people.

—H. W. Sylvester

22 ◆ Don't admire people for their wealth but for the creative and generous ways they put it to use.

Try not to become a man of success, but rather try to become a man of values.

—Albert Einstein

A Coincidence?

I was very proud of my daughter Emily. At only nine years old, she had been carefully saving her allowance money all year and trying to earn extra money by doing small jobs around the neighborhood. Emily was determined to save enough to buy a girl's mountain bike, an item for which she'd been longing, and she'd been faithfully putting her money away since the beginning of the year.

"How are you doing, honey?" I asked soon after Thanksgiving. I knew she had hoped to have all the money she needed by the end of the year.

"I have forty-nine dollars, Daddy," she said. "I'm not sure if I'm going to make it."

"You've worked so hard," I said encouragingly. "Keep it up. But you know that you can have your pick from my bicycle collection."

"Thanks, Daddy. But your bikes are so old."

I smiled to myself because I knew she was right. As a collector of vintage bicycles, all my girls' bikes were 1950s models—not the kind a kid would choose today.

When the Christmas season arrived, Emily and I went comparison shopping, and she saw several less expensive bikes for which she thought she'd have to settle. As we left one store, she noticed a Salvation Army volunteer ringing his bell by a big kettle. "Can we give them something, Daddy?" she asked.

"Sorry, Em, I'm out of change," I replied.

Emily continued to work hard all through December, and it seemed she might make her goal after all. Then suddenly one day, she came downstairs to the kitchen and made an announcement to her mother.

"Mom," she said hesitantly, "you know all the money I've been saving?"

"Yes, dear," smiled my wife, Diane.

"God told me to give it to the poor people."

Diane knelt down to Emily's level. "That's a very kind thought, sweetheart. But you've been saving all year. Maybe you could give some of it."

Emily shook her head vigorously. "God said all."

When we saw she was serious, we gave her various suggestions about where she could contribute. But Emily had received specific instructions, and so one cold Sunday morning before Christmas, with little fanfare, she handed her total savings of $58 to a surprised and grateful Salvation Army volunteer.

Moved by Emily's selflessness, I suddenly noticed that a local car dealer was collecting used bicycles to refurbish and give to poor children for Christmas. And I realized that if my nine-year-old daughter could give away all her money, I could certainly give up one bike from my collection.

As I picked up a shiny but old-fashioned kid's bike from the line in the garage, it seemed as if a second bicycle in the line took on a glow. Should I give a second bike? No, certainly the one would be enough.

But as I got to my car, I couldn't shake the feeling that I should donate that second bike as well. And if Emily could follow heavenly instructions, I decided I could, too. I turned back and loaded the second bike into the trunk, then took off for the dealership.

When I delivered the bikes, the car dealer thanked me and said, "You're making two kids very happy, Mr. Koper. And here are your tickets."

"Tickets?" I asked.

"Yes. For each bike donated, we're giving away one chance to win a brand new men's 21-speed mountain bike from a local bike shop. So here are your tickets for two chances."

Why wasn't I surprised when it was the second ticket that won the prize bike? "I can't believe you won!" laughed Diane, delighted.

"I didn't," I said. "It's pretty clear that Emily did."

And why wasn't I surprised when the bike dealer happily substituted a gorgeous new girl's mountain bike for the man's bike advertised?

Coincidence? Maybe. I like to think it was God's way of rewarding a little girl for a sacrifice beyond her years—while giving her dad a lesson in charity and the power of the Lord.

—Ed Koper

23 ◆ Get involved with Habitat for Humanity and help build housing for the poor. Call 1-800-HABITAT.

We dwell in the shelter of one another.

—IRISH PROVERB

24 ◆ Let your children observe you being generous to those in need.

Being considerate of others will take you and your children further in life than any college or professional degree.

—MARIAN WRIGHT EDELMAN

I don't know what your destiny will be, but one thing I know: The only ones among you who will be truly happy are those who will have sought and found how to serve.

—Albert Schweitzer

25 ◆ Volunteer to help at your city's Special Olympics.

If you want to lift yourself up, lift up someone else.

—Booker T. Washington

26 ◆ Never decide to do nothing just because you can do only a little. Do what you can.

I am only one, but still I am one;
I cannot do everything, but still I can do
 something;
And just because I cannot do everything,
I will not refuse to do the something
 that I can do.

—Edward E. Hale

27 ◆ Always put something in the collection plate.

He who is not generous with what he has deceives himself when he thinks he would be more generous if he had more.

—W. S. PLUMER

28 ◆ When a friend is in need, help him without his having to ask.

Those who give when they are asked to have waited too long.

—KOBI YAMADA

The biggest disease today is not leprosy or tuberculosis, but rather the feeling of being unwanted, uncared for, and deserted by everybody. We can cure physical diseases with medicine, but the only cure for loneliness, despair, and hopelessness is love.

—Mother Teresa

A Time of Need

Many years ago two boys were working their way through Stanford University. Their funds got desperately low, and the idea came to them to engage the famous pianist Ignacy Paderewski for a piano recital. They would use the funds to help pay their board and tuition.

The great pianist's manager asked for a guarantee of $2,000. The guarantee was a lot of money in those days, but the boys agreed and proceeded to promote the concert. They worked hard, only to find that they had grossed only $1,600.

After the concert the two boys told the great artist the bad news. They gave him the entire $1,600, along with a promissory note for $400, explaining that they would earn the amount at the earliest possible moment and send the money to him. It looked like the end of their college careers.

"No, boys," replied Paderewski, "that won't do." Then, tearing the note in two, he returned the money to them as well. "Now," he told them, "take out of this $1,600 all of your expenses, and keep for each of you 10 percent of the balance for your work. I will be satisfied with the amount remaining."

The years rolled by—World War I came and went. Paderewski, now premier of Poland, was trying to feed thousands of starving people in his native land. The only person in the world who could help him was Herbert Hoover, who was in charge of the U.S. Food and Relief Bureau. Hoover responded and soon thousands of tons of food were sent to Poland.

After the starving people were fed, Paderewski journeyed to Paris to thank Mr. Hoover for the relief he had sent to him.

"That's all right, Mr. Paderewski," was Hoover's reply. "Besides, you don't remember it, but you helped me once when I was a student at college, and I was in trouble."

—As cited in *The Best of Bits & Pieces*

29 ◆ Never remind someone of a kindness or act of generosity you have shown him or her. Bestow a favor and then forget it.

You must give time to your fellow men—even if it's a little thing, do something for others—something for which you get no pay but the privilege of doing it.

—Albert Schweitzer

30 ◆ Contribute at least five percent of your income to charity.

God does not comfort us to make us comfortable, but to make us comforters.

—J. H. Lovett

31 ◆ Be an example of what you want to see more of in the world.

The example of great and pure individuals is the only thing that can lead us to noble thoughts and deeds.

—Albert Einstein

32 ◆ Measure your wealth by what you'd have left if you lost all your money.

If all I'm remembered for is being a good basketball player, then I've done a bad job with the rest of my life.

—Isiah Thomas

Homework

What you give will always afford you more pleasure than what you get. It's a simple truth, but when you live by it, generosity will become a way of life you *want* to follow instead of something you feel you *have* to do. You will actually find yourself looking for ways to practice generosity. Here are a few ideas for today:

- Leave a quarter where a child can find it.
- Skip a meal and give what you would have spent to a street person.
- Offer to pay for parking and tolls when you ride with someone.
- Buy whatever kids are selling on card tables in their front yards.
- Make a generous contribution to diabetes research.

Simple Pleasures

Nearest and Dearest

Anne Morrow Lindbergh, in her classic bestseller *Gift From the Sea*, observes, "It is not the life of simplicity, but the life of multiplicity that the wise men warn us of. It leads not to unification, but to fragmentation. It does not bring grace, it destroys the soul."

Herein lies a beautiful truth: all of us experience that which is nearest and dearest to our heart in our own way, our own place. Just hearing the words *porch swing*, *rocking chair*, *bubble bath*, or *back rub* can stall my heartbeat just a bit and invoke a sigh. It is cause to pause.

Life invites us to pause along the way and linger in its simple pleasures—sunrises, sunsets, sunflower fields, kisses hello, kisses goodbye, freshly baked bread, homemade pies, stained glass windows, tulip festivals, caramel apples, bathing in moonlight, falling asleep to the sound of crickets, whistling, hearing "I love you," saying "I love you," being tickled, singing in the shower, watching loved ones slumber, moseying around farmer's markets, wishing on falling stars, being hugged, sleeping with old quilts and embroidered pillow cases, hearing three-year-olds sing the ABC's, seeing red cardinals against white snow, smelling cotton sheets fresh from the clothesline, rocking babies, cozying up in flannel pajamas and warm slippers, seeing a dog's tail wag, eating meals together as a family, seeing potted violets on window sills, playing the harmonica, hearing a rooster's call at daybreak, admiring Jack Frost's artwork on winter window panes, sipping flavored coffee, sleeping late, finding hand-written letters in one's mailbox, reading bedtime stories, saying bedtime prayers, playing "This Little Piggy" on a child's toes, hearing the sound of the ocean in sea shells brought home from faraway vacations, wearing old jeans, having a new idea, sleeping with a clear conscience, hearing neighbors holler hello from across the yard.

Life is beckoning each of us. What are we waiting for?

1 ◆ Plant flowers every spring.

People from a planet without flowers would think we must be mad with joy the whole time to have such things about us.

—IRIS MURDOCH

2 ◆ Learn to make great spaghetti sauce.

The most indispensable ingredient of all good home cooking: love for those you are cooking for.

—SOPHIA LOREN

3 ◆ Think big thoughts, but relish small pleasures.

Blessed is the man who can enjoy the small things, the common beauties, the little day-by-day events: sunshine on the fields, birds on the bough, breakfast, dinner, supper, a friend passing by. So many people who go afield to search for happiness have left it behind them back home sitting on the front porch.

—David Grayson

4 ◆ Have a dog.

No matter how little money and how few possessions you own, having a dog makes you rich.

—Louis Sabin

Finding a way to live the simple life today is man's most complicated task.

—HENRY A. COURTNEY

5 ◆ Put a lot of little marsh-mallows in your hot chocolate.

My tongue is smiling.

—Abigail Trillin

6 ◆ Stop and watch a farmer plowing a field.

To watch the corn grow or the
blossoms set;
To draw hard breath over the
ploughshare or spade;
To read, to think, to love, to pray
Are the things that make men happy.

—John Ruskin

7 ◆ Learn to play a musical instrument.

I think I should have no other mortal wants if I could always have plenty of music. It seems to infuse strength into my limbs and ideas into my brain. Life seems to go on without effort when I am filled with music.

—GEORGE ELIOT

8 ◆ Laugh loudly.

Laughter is the sensation of feeling good all over but showing it primarily in one spot.

—JOSH BILLINGS

9 ◆ Keep a daily journal.

If your life is worth living, it's worth recording.

—MARILYN GREY

10 ◆ Keep a couple of your favorite inspirational books by your bedside.

Only one hour in the normal day is more pleasurable than the hour spent in bed with a book before going to sleep, and that is the hour spent in bed with a book after being called in the morning.

—ROSE MACAULAY

. . . clocks ticking . . .
and Mama's sunflowers. And
food and coffee. And new-
ironed dresses and hot baths
. . . and sleeping and wak-
ing up. Oh, earth, you're
too wonderful for anybody
to realize you.

—THORNTON WILDER, *OUR TOWN*

The Miser

A man had a large sum of gold, which he buried in the ground, coming to the spot every day to look at it and count it piece by piece. He made so many trips that a thief, who had been observing him, guessed what it was that the man had hidden, and one night quietly dug up the treasure and made off with it.

When the man discovered his loss, he was overcome with grief and despair. He groaned and cried and tore at his hair.

A neighbor, seeing him, said, "Do not grieve so. Bury a stone in the hole and fancy it is the gold. It will serve you just as well, for when the gold was there you made no use of it."

—AESOP

11 ◆ Spend some time alone.

When we cannot bear to be alone, it means we do not properly value or appreciate the only companion we will have from birth to death—ourselves.

—EDA LESHAN

12 ◆ Buy vegetables from truck farmers who advertise with hand-lettered signs.

It's difficult to think anything but pleasant thoughts while eating a home-grown tomato.

—LEWIS GRIZZARD

13 ◆ Don't overlook life's small joys while searching for the big ones.

Savor life's tiny delights—a crackling fire, a glorious sunset, a hug from a child, a walk with a loved one, a kiss behind the ear.

—JOHN ANTHONY

14 ◆ Buy a bird feeder and hang it so that you can see it from your kitchen window.

We judge the song of the bird not by its musical quality nor even by its creativeness, but by its effect on the human spirit.

—LEN EISERER

15 ◆ Learn three knock-knock jokes so that you will always be ready to entertain children.

Laughter is the best communion of all.

—ROBERT FULGHUM

16 ◆ Don't let your possessions possess you.

The more you get, the more you got to take care of.

—ALICE DORMANN

17 ◆ Watch less TV.

There are days when any electrical appliance in the house, including the vacuum cleaner, seems to offer more entertainment possibilities than the TV set.

—Harriet Van Horne

18 ◆ Take Sunday afternoon drives through the country.

I think it ticks God off if you pass the color purple in a field somewhere and don't notice it.

—Alice Walker

19 ◆ Join a choir.

Do not be afraid to use what talents you possess, for how silent the woods would be if no birds sang except those which sang best.

—HENRY VAN DYKE

20 ◆ Every so often watch *Sesame Street.*

We are children only once, but we can keep the child in us forever.

—BROCK TULLY

Sensory Deprivation

I want to go dancing and wear a dress that swirls and floats around me, and laugh.

I want to feel the shimmer of silk as it glides over my arms and down my body, the joy of fingering its whispery softness.

I want to sleep in my own bed and luxuriate in the cool crispness of clean sheets, and rest my head on my own soft pillow. And go to sleep when I want to, with all the lights out, and wake up when I'm ready.

I want to stretch out on my couch under my blue-plaid afghan and listen as my favorite music seeps from the speakers and into my being, watering the parched landscape of my soul.

I want to sit on my porch and sip hot coffee from my stoneware mug, and read the newspaper, and hear the dog bark at blowing leaves and trespassing squirrels.

I want to answer the phone and call my friends and family and talk until we catch up on all the words we've saved for each other, and laugh.

I want to hear the train hoot through Loveland, the gravel crunch in the driveway, and car doors slam as friends come to visit. And the tinkle and clink of silverware on china, the hiss and gurgle of the coffee maker.

I want to feel my bare feet on the cool whiteness of my kitchen floor, and the soft blueness of my bedroom carpet.

I want to see the colors, all of them, every color ever spun into existence. And white, true white, pristine and unblemished. And acres of green trees, and miles of yellow-ribbon highways, and yards of Christmas lights. And the moon.

I want to smell bacon sizzling, a steak broiling, Thanksgiving dinner and my father's tomato vines. And fresh laundry. And the ocean.

But more than all of this, I want to stand in the doorway of my son's room and watch him sleep. And hear him get up in the morning and see him come home at night. And touch his face and comb my fingers through his hair, and ride in his truck and eat his grilled cheese sandwiches.

And watch him grow and laugh and play and eat and drive and live. Mostly, mostly, live. And put my arms around him and hold him until he laughs and says, "Mom, that's enough!"

And then be free to do it again.

—Deborah E. Hill
WRITTEN WHILE IN PRISON

He is richest who is
content with the least.

—SOCRATES

21 ◆ Visit a pet store every once in a while and watch the children watch the animals.

All animals except man know that the ultimate joy of life is to enjoy it.

—Samuel Butler

22 ◆ Lie on your back and look at the stars.

Be glad of life because it gives you a chance to love and to play and to look up at the stars.

—Henry Van Dyke

23 ◆ Learn to make great chili.

Home is a place where a pot of fresh soup simmers gently on the hob, filling the kitchen with soft aromas . . . and filling your heart, and later your tummy, with joy.

—KEITH FLOYD

24 ◆ Rake a big pile of leaves every fall and jump in it with someone you love.

When we recall the past, we find it is the simplest things—not the great occasions—that in retrospect give off the greatest glow of happiness.

—BOB HOPE

25 ◆ Daydream.

Within your heart, keep one still, secret spot where dreams may go.

—LOUISE DRISCOLL

26 ◆ Take time to smell the roses.

One of the tragic things I know about human nature is that all of us tend to put off living. We are all dreaming of some magical rose garden over the horizon—instead of enjoying the roses that are blooming outside our windows today.

—DALE CARNEGIE

27 ◆ At the movies, buy Junior Mints and sprinkle them on your popcorn.

It isn't the big pleasures that count the most; it's making a great deal out of the little ones.

—JEAN WEBSTER

28 ◆ Sing in the shower.

The ordinary acts we practice every day at home are of more importance to the soul than their simplicity might suggest.

—THOMAS MOORE

How Much Is Enough?

The rich industrialist from the North was horrified to find the southern fisherman lying lazily beside his boat, smoking a pipe.

"Why aren't you out fishing?" said the industrialist.

"Because I have caught enough fish for the day," said the fisherman.

"Why don't you catch some more?"

"What would I do with them?"

"You could earn more money," was the industrialist's reply. "With that you could have a motor fixed to your boat and go into deeper waters and catch more fish. Then you would make enough to buy nylon nets. These would bring you more fish and more money. Soon you would have enough money to own two boats . . . maybe even a fleet of boats. Then you would be a rich man like me."

"What would I do then?" asked the fisherman.

"Then you could really enjoy life."

"What do you think I am doing right now?"

—Anthony de Mello

29 ◆ Enjoy a bubble bath illuminated by vanilla-scented candles.

There must be quite a few things a hot bath won't cure, but I don't know of many of them.

—SYLVIA PLATH

30 ◆ Begin each day with your favorite music.

Music is love in search of a word.

—SIDNEY LANIER

The foolish man seeks happiness in the distance, the wise man grows it under his feet.

—James Oppenheim

31 ◆ Watch a sunset.

If I don't celebrate the exquisiteness of each day, I've lost something I will never get back.

—Sally P. Karioth

32 ◆ Always have something beautiful in sight, even if it's just a daisy in a jelly glass.

The beauty of the world around us is only according to what we, ourselves, bring to it.

—Ralph Waldo Emerson

33 ◆ Every once in a while, take the scenic route.

I believe the nicest and sweetest days are not those on which anything very splendid or wonderful or exciting happens, but just those days that bring simple little pleasures, following one another softly, like pearls slipping off of a string.

—Lucy Maud Montgomery

34 ◆ Count your blessings.

Every morning I wake up and say, "Dear Lord, I don't want anything better; just send me more of the same."

—Kitty Hart

35 ◆ Forget the Joneses.

When will you know you have enough, and what will you do then?

—Barbara De Angelis

36 ◆ Learn to make something beautiful with your hands.

Every child is an artist. The problem is to remain an artist once he grows up.

—Pablo Picasso

A Flight of Geese

Yesterday I watched a huge flight of geese winging their way south through one of those panoramic sunsets that color the entire sky for a few moments. I saw them as I leaned against the lion statue in front of the Chicago Art Institute, where I was watching the Christmas shoppers hurry along Michigan Avenue. When I lowered my gaze, I noticed that a bag lady, standing a few feet away, had also been watching the geese. Our eyes met and we smiled—silently acknowledging the fact that we had shared a marvelous sight, a symbol of the mystery of the struggle to survive. I overheard the lady talking to herself as she shuffled away. Her words, "God spoils me," were startling.

Was the lady, this street derelict, being facetious? No. I believe the sight of the geese had shattered, however briefly, the harsh reality of her own struggle. I realized later that moments such as this one sustained her; it was the way she survived the indignity of the street. Her smile was real.

The sight of the geese was her Christmas present. It was proof God existed. It was all she needed.

I envy her.

—Fred Lloyd Cochran

There must be more to life than having everything.

—Maurice Sendak

37 ◆ Regardless of your age, occasionally stop at a public playground and ride on the swings.

It is a happy talent to know how to play.

—RALPH WALDO EMERSON

38 ◆ Rock a child to sleep to discover a deep satisfaction and peace.

I am beginning to learn that it is the sweet, simple things of life which are the real ones after all.

—LAURA INGALLS WILDER

39 ◆ Take a nap on Sunday afternoon.

For fast acting relief try slowing down.

—LILY TOMLIN

40 ◆ Read the comics.

The most wasted of all days is the one during which you have not laughed.

—NICOLAS CHAMFORT

41 ◆ Life will sometimes hand you a magical moment. Savor it.

We do not remember days. We remember moments.

—Cesare Pavese

42 ◆ Always take your vacation time.

There are two things to aim at in life: first, to get what you want; and, after that, to enjoy it. Only the wisest of mankind achieves the second.

—Logan Pearsall Smith

Year by year the complexities of this spinning world grow more bewildering, and so each year we need all the more to seek peace and comfort in joyful simplicities.

Woman's Home Companion
—December, 1935

43 ◆ Never acquire just one kitten. Two are a lot more fun and no more trouble.

You can't look at a sleeping cat and be tense.

—JANE PAULEY

44 ◆ Savor every day.

To me, every hour of the light and dark is a miracle,
Every cubic inch of space is a miracle.

—WALT WHITMAN

Homework

As you dash, crash, zig, and zag your way through stressful schedules and impossible deadlines, it is easy to forget that the satisfaction and fulfillment you seek can often be found where you *are* and with what you *already possess*. Here are six simple activities that are sure to soothe your spirit and delight your senses.

- Put a love note in your child's lunch box.
- Wave at children on school buses.
- Buy your mother a book you think she would enjoy.
- Purchase the soundtrack from the movie *Meet Joe Black* and enjoy Israel Kamakawiwo'ole singing "Somewhere Over the Rainbow/What a Wonderful World" accompanied only by ukulele. It's uncommonly beautiful and inspiring.
- Sweeten your oatmeal with real maple syrup.
- Warm your underwear in the dryer for a few minutes before putting it on.

Attitude

It's Our Choice

We've seen it many times. A cat is backed into a corner by the neighborhood dog. The cat hikes up its back, magically doubling in size, hisses like a snake, and claws the air like a deranged lioness. The dog suddenly decides it would be more prudent to go chase squirrels in the park.

What's going on? The cat has acquired an *attitude*. There's no way it can go toe-to-toe with a seventy-five-pound Doberman, but by jimminy it sure *looks* as if it can, and that qualifies as a successful encounter.

We all face snarling dogs every day. How we choose to deal with them determines the quality of our lives. The attitudes we adopt are always superior to facts and situations. Like the cat backed into the corner, we can decide to be bigger than our circumstances and stronger than our fears.

I often wear a white baseball-style cap with the word ATTITUDE across the front in big blue letters. I wear it hoping it might provide inspiration to me and to anyone who might notice it. And people often do. I see their eyes reading the single word; I almost hear the gears in their head clicking with recognition: "Yes. Attitude. ATTITUDE! I need to remember that." Such a simple decision, so immediate a result.

When I straighten my cap, I'm reminded that my attitude probably needs adjusting, too.

1 ◆ Remember that you can miss a lot of good things in life by having the wrong attitude.

And life is what we make it, always has been, always will be.

—GRANDMA MOSES

2 ◆ Become the most positive and enthusiastic person you know.

It is a gift to be able to paint a particular picture or to carve a statue, and so to make a few objects beautiful; but it is far more glorious to carve and paint the very atmosphere and medium through which we look. To affect the quality of the day—that is the highest of the arts.

—HENRY DAVID THOREAU

3 ◆ Forgive quickly.

My dog and cat have taught me a great lesson in life . . . shed a lot.

—Susan Carlson

4 ◆ Spend your life lifting people up, not putting people down.

Running down people is a bad habit, whether you are a gossip or a motorist.

—Anonymous

5 ◆ Make the most of the best and the least of the worst.

Every life has its dark and cheerful hours. Happiness comes from choosing which to remember.

—ANONYMOUS

6 ◆ Remember the three powerful resources you always have available to you: love, prayer, and forgiveness.

At night I turn my problems over to God. He's going to be up all night anyway.

—CARRIE WESTINGSON

7 ◆ Remember that happiness comes as a result of putting others before yourself.

Why aren't you happy? It's because ninety-nine percent of everything you do, and think, and say, is for yourself.

—Wu Wei Wu

8 ◆ Be cheerful, even when you don't feel like it.

Some days there won't be a song in your heart. Sing anyway.

—Emory Austin

A man without a sense of humor is like a wagon without springs—he is jolted disagreeably by every little pebble in the road.

—HENRY WARD BEECHER

9 ◆ Don't forget that one minute of anger denies you sixty seconds of happiness.

You live more fully once you realize that any time spent being unhappy is wasted.

—Ruth E. Renkl

10 ◆ When you arrive at your place of work in the morning, let the first thing you say brighten everyone's day.

Happiness is contagious. Be a carrier.

—Robert Orben

11 ◆ Don't whine.

If you have not slept, or if you have a headache, or leprosy, or scatia, or thunder-stroke, I beseech you, by all angels, to hold your peace, and not pollute the morning.

—Ralph Waldo Emerson

12 ◆ It's O.K. to feel sorry for yourself; just don't let it last for more than five minutes.

What the mind dwells on, expands.

—Norman Vincent Peale

13 ◆ Be happy with what you have while working for what you want.

So much has been given to me, I have no time to ponder over that which has been denied.

—HELEN KELLER

14 ◆ Don't take good friends, good health, or a good marriage for granted.

Just think how happy you'd be if you lost everything and everyone you have right now, and then, somehow got everything back again.

—KOBI YAMADA

Attitude

I believe the single most significant decision I can make on a day-to-day basis is my choice of attitude. It is more important than my past, my education, my bankroll, my successes or failures, fame or pain, what other people think of me or say about me, my circumstances, or my position. Attitude keeps me going or cripples my progress. . . . It alone fuels my fire or assaults my hope. When my attitude is right, there's no barrier too high, no valley too deep, no dream too extreme, no challenge too great for me.

—Charles Swindoll

15 ◆ **Whether it is life or a horse that throws you, get right back on.**

How a person masters his fate is more important than what his fate is.

—Wilhelm von Humboldt

16 ◆ **Be modest. A lot was accomplished before you were born.**

I never forgot for a day, or for an hour, or for a minute, that I climbed to my position on the backs of the courageous African-American men and women who went before me.

—Colin L. Powell

There is the positive side
and the negative side and
at every moment I decide.

—WILLIAM JAMES

17 ◆ Every problem has two handles. You can grab it by the handle of fear or by the handle of hope.

Nothing in life is so hard that you can't make it easier by the way you take it.

—ELLEN GLASGOW

18 ◆ Look for the opportunity that's hidden in every adversity.

The pessimist sees the difficulty in every opportunity; the optimist, the opportunity in every difficulty.

—L. P. JACKS

19 ◆ Don't expect life to be fair.

If I could wish for my life to be perfect, it would be tempting but I would have to decline, for life would no longer teach me anything.

—Allyson Jones

20 ◆ Never forget that you can sit and worry until you are physically ill, but worry doesn't change things. Action does.

You can't wring your hands and roll up your sleeves at the same time.

—Anonymous

21 ◆ Apply this simple rule to your conversations: If you wouldn't write it down and sign it, don't say it.

Little said is soonest mended.

—George Wither

22 ◆ Keep in mind that the desire to have a positive impact on the lives of others has an even bigger impact on your own life.

The game of life is the game of boomerangs. Our thoughts, words, and deeds return to us—sooner or later—with astounding accuracy.

—Florence Shinn

23 ◆ Remember that no situation is so bad that losing your temper won't make it worse.

Speak when you are angry and you will make the best speech you will ever regret.

—AMBROSE BIERCE

24 ◆ Don't allow another person's disposition to determine yours. No matter what the circumstances are, always react with class.

He who smiles rather than rages is always the stronger.

—JAPANESE PROVERB

Promise Yourself

To be so strong that nothing can disturb your peace of mind.
To talk health, happiness, and prosperity to every person you meet.
To make all your friends feel that there is something in them.
To look at the sunny side of everything and make your optimism come true.
To think only of the best, to work only for the best, and to expect only the best.
To be just as enthusiastic about the success of others as you are about your own.
To forget the mistakes of the past and press on to the greater achievements of the future.
To wear a cheerful countenance at all times and give every living creature you meet a smile.
To give so much time to the improvement of yourself that you have no time to criticize others.
To be too large for worry, too noble for anger, too strong for fear, and too happy to permit the presence of trouble.

—The Optimist Creed
by Christian D. Larson

25 ◆ Don't carry a grudge.

. . . While you're carrying the grudge the other guy's out dancing.

—Buddy Hackett

26 ◆ Make allowances for other people's faults as readily as you do for your own.

If you do not learn how to love and forgive others, everywhere you go, you are going to suffer.

—Eknath Easwaran

27 ◆ Never underestimate the power of laughter.

If you could choose one characteristic that would get you through life, choose a sense of humor.

—JENNIFER JAMES

28 ◆ Remember that it may be all right to be content with what you have, but never with what you are.

There's always room for improvement—it's the biggest room in the house.

—LOUISE HEATH LEBER

God asks no man whether he will accept life. That is not the choice. You must take it. The only question is how.

—HENRY WARD BEECHER

29 ◆ Remember that the more content you are with yourself, the fewer material things you need.

Riches come not from an abundance of worldly goods, but from a contented mind.

—Mohammed

30 ◆ Don't get too big for your britches.

Check your ego at the door.

—Quincy Jones

31 ◆ Never underestimate the potential and power of the human spirit.

Although the world is full of suffering, it's also full of the overcoming of it.

—HELEN KELLER

32 ◆ Share the credit.

There is no such thing as a self-made man. You will reach your goals only with the help of others.

—GEORGE SHINN

The greater part of our happiness or misery depends on our mental disposition and not on our circumstances.

—MARTHA WASHINGTON

33 ◆ Learn to laugh at yourself.

Blessed is he who has learned how to laugh at himself, for he shall never cease to be entertained.

—JOHN BOWELL

34 ◆ Your mind can hold only one thought at a time. Make it a positive one.

Finally, brethren, whatever things are true, whatever things are noble, whatever things are just, whatever things are pure, whatever things are lovely, whatever things are of good report, if there is any virtue and if there is anything praiseworthy—meditate on these things.

—PHILIPPIANS 4:8

What Do You See?

This story has been retold countless times in countless ways over many centuries. It happened like this:

A traveler approached a great, walled city. Before entering its gates, he stopped to talk with an old man seated beneath a tree.

"What are the people like in this city?" asked the traveler.

"How were the people from where you came?" wondered the old man.

"A terrible lot," grumbled the traveler. "Mean, miserable, and detestable in all respects."

"You will find them here the same," responded the old man.

A second traveler soon happened by. He, too, was on his way to the great city and stopped to ask the old man about the people he would soon meet there.

The old man repeated the question he asked the first traveler. "How were the people from where you came?"

To this the second traveler answered, "They were fine people. Generous, kind, compassionate."

"You will find them here the same," observed the old man.

35 ◆ Take responsibility for every area of your life. Stop blaming others.

We are taught you must blame your father, your sisters, your brothers, the school, the teachers—you can blame anyone, but never blame yourself because it's never your fault. But it's *ALWAYS* your fault, because if you wanted to change, you're the one who has got to change. It's as simple as that, isn't it?

—Katherine Hepburn

36 ◆ Evaluate yourself by your own standards, not someone else's.

Let us not try to be the best or worst for others, but let us make every effort to be the best for ourselves.

—Marcus Garvey

37 ◆ Memorize this statement by coach Lou Holtz: "Life is 10 percent what happens to me and 90 percent how I react to it."

A happy person is not a person in a certain set of circumstances, but rather a person with a certain set of attitudes.

—HUGH DOWNS

38 ◆ Count your blessings.

For today and its blessings, I owe the world an attitude of gratitude.

—CLARENCE E. HODGES

39 ◆ Learn to be comfortable with problems; that's where personal growth and opportunities lie.

The chief pang of most trials is not so much the actual suffering itself as our spirit of resistance to it.

—Jean Nicolas Groll

40 ◆ Remember that if you look for the worst in life and in people, you'll find it. But if you look for the best, you'll find that instead.

What you see reflects your thinking, and your thinking but reflects the choice of what you want to see.

—*A Course in Miracles*

Homework

We all know the importance of keeping a positive attitude. But some days it's hard to find the energy to "crank it up." Here are a few suggestions you might want to try when your attitude needs a little boost. You'll be surprised at the big difference a little change can make.

- Encourage and compliment someone who is not expecting it.
- Say something positive as early as possible tomorrow morning.
- Smile when you answer the phone. The caller will hear it in your voice.
- Improve your attitude by improving your posture.
- Arrive five minutes early for appointments.
- The next time you're tempted to say, "It'll never work," say instead, "Who knows? It just might."

Marriage

The Promise

Whether spoken in a sanctuary, a garden, or before a Justice of the Peace, marriage vows take only moments to exchange. Yet these words, eloquent or simple, transcend circumstances in their commitment to love no matter what and for always. Two become one. "I" becomes "us." "Me" becomes "we."

To have *and* to hold. In sickness *and* in health. To love *and* to cherish. *And* is such a simple little word. Or is it?

The *and*s in the marriage vow connect the ebbs and flows of life that will surely come, for such are the seasons of our existence. In these promises the deepest truths of life are laid bare, requiring much more than an agreement by the bride and groom, invoking instead the need for a total commitment.

Perhaps it is clear at the moment of "I do," or perhaps it will become evident in the days and years ahead as the couple seeks to fulfill the promise they offered one another. Love, ultimately, is more than a romantic feeling; it is a decision, a choice, a conscious act of the will—entailing compromise, understanding, and forgiveness. It means standing firm and holding fast through the difficult and trying times when "better" and "richer" and "health" seem to be hiding under the sofa. But all is made right if they love *and* cherish and remain true to their commitment.

1 ◆ Choose your life's mate carefully. From this one decision will come ninety percent of all your happiness or misery.

What greater thing is there for two human souls than to feel that they are joined for life—to strengthen each other in all labor, to rest on each other in all sorrow, to minister to each other in all pain, to be one with each other in silent, unspeakable memories at the moment of the last parting.

—GEORGE ELIOT

2 ◆ Marry only for love.

Now join your hands, and with your hands your hearts.

—WILLIAM SHAKESPEARE

Nobody has ever measured,
not even poets, how much
the heart can hold.

—ZELDA FITZGERALD

3 ◆ Every day look for some small way to improve your marriage.

Give me your hands; receive you her, you him; be plighted with a love that grows as you decay.

—William Shakespeare

4 ◆ Be romantic.

One of the great illusions of our time is that love is self-seeking. It is not. Love must be fed and nurtured, constantly renewed. That demands ingenuity and consideration, but first and foremost, it demands time.

—David R. Mace

5 ◆ Make your wedding anniversary an all-day celebration.

The question is asked, "Is there anything more beautiful in life than a boy and a girl clasping clean hands and pure hearts in the path of marriage? Can there be anything more beautiful than young love?" And the answer is given: "Yes, there is a more beautiful thing. It is the spectacle of an old man and an old woman finishing their journey together on that path. Their hands are gnarled, but still clasped; their faces seamed, but still radiant; their hearts are physically bowed and tired, but still strong with love and devotion for one another. Yes, there is a more beautiful thing than young love. Old love."

—A. L. Alexander

6 ◆ Remember that children, marriages, and flower gardens reflect the kind of care they get.

The grass is not greener on the other side of the fence. It is the greenest where nurtured and cared for. If your grass is not green, what are you doing—or not doing—to have it that way?

—Wedding Ceremony Sermon

7 ◆ Become your spouse's best friend.

Two souls with but a single thought; two hearts that beat as one.

—Von Munch Bellinghausen

If ever two were one, then surely we.

—ANNE BRADSTREET

8 ◆ Be the first to forgive.

A wise man will make haste to forgive because he knows the full value of time and will not suffer it to pass in unnecessary pain.

—RAMBLER

9 ◆ Remember that a woman never gets tired of hearing these words: "I love you," "I cherish you," "I'm so lucky to have found you."

Man's love is of man's life apart;
'Tis woman's whole existence.

—LORD BYRON

10 ◆ Put a love note in your husband's luggage before he leaves on a trip.

More than kisses, letters mingle souls.

—John Donne

11 ◆ Remember that to love and to be loved is the greatest joy in the world.

The most precious possession that ever comes to a man in this world is a woman's heart.

—Josiah G. Holland

The Weinsberg Wives

The wives who lived within the walls of the Weinsberg Castle in Germany were well aware of the riches the castle held: gold, silver, jewels, and wealth beyond belief.

Then the day came in 1141 when all their treasure was threatened. An enemy army had surrounded the castle and demanded the fortress, the fortune, and the lives of the men within. There was nothing to do but surrender.

Although the conquering commander had set a condition for the safe release of all women and children, the wives of Weinsberg refused to leave without having one of their own conditions met as well: they demanded that they be allowed to fill their arms with as many possessions as they could carry out with them. Knowing that the women couldn't possibly make a dent in the massive fortune, their request was honored.

When the castle gates opened, the army outside was brought to tears. Each woman had carried out her husband.

The wives of Weinsberg, indeed, were well aware of the riches the castle held.

12 ◆ **Create a little signal only your wife knows so that you can show her you love her across a crowded room.**

There was nothing remote or mysterious here—just something private. The only secret was the ancient communication between two people.

—Eudora Welty

13 ◆ **Never waste an opportunity to tell someone you love them.**

I like not only to be loved, but to be told that I am loved; the realm of silence is large enough beyond the grave.

—George Eliot

A successful marriage requires falling in love many times, always with the same person.

—MIGNON MCLAUGHLIN

14 ◆ Let your children see you do things for your wife that let them know how much you love and treasure her.

Happy marriages begin when we marry the ones we love, and they blossom when we love the ones we marry.

—Tom Mullen

15 ◆ Respect each other's need for privacy.

Constant togetherness is fine—but only for Siamese twins.

—Victoria Billings

16 ◆ Remember that a successful marriage depends on two things: (1) finding the right person, and (2) being the right person.

We believe that we are hurt when we don't receive love. But that is not what hurts us. Our pain comes from when we do not *give* love. We function most powerfully when we are giving love. The world has led us to believe that our well-being is dependent on other people loving us. But this is the kind of upside-down thinking that has caused so many of our problems. The truth is that our well-being is dependent on our giving love. It is not about what comes back; it is about what goes out.

—Alan Cohen

17 ◆ Save an evening a week for just you and your wife.

To keep a fire burning brightly there's one easy rule: keep the logs together, near enough to keep warm and far enough apart for breathing room. Good fire, good marriage, same rule.

—MARNIE REED CROWEL

18 ◆ No matter how angry you get with your spouse, never sleep apart.

Do not let the sun go down on your wrath.

—EPHESIANS 4:26

The Gift of the Magi

Della finished her cry and attended to her cheeks with the powder rag. She stood by the window and looked out dully at a gray cat walking a gray fence in a gray backyard. Tomorrow would be Christmas Day, and she had only $1.87 with which to buy Jim a present. She had been saving every penny she could for months, with this result. Twenty dollars a week doesn't go far. Expenses had been greater than she had calculated. They always are. Only $1.87 to buy a present for Jim. Her Jim. Many a happy hour she had spent planning for something nice for him. Something fine and rare and sterling—something just a little bit near to being worthy of the honor of being owned by him. . . .

Now there were two possessions of the James Dillingham Youngs in which they both took a mighty pride. One was Jim's gold watch that had been his father's and his grandfather's. The other was Della's hair. Had the Queen of Sheba lived in the flat across the airshaft, Della would have let her hair hang out the window some day to dry just to depreciate Her Majesty's jewels and gifts. Had King Solomon been the janitor, with all his treasures piled up in the basement, Jim would have pulled out his watch every time he passed, just to see him pluck at his beard from envy.

So now Della's beautiful hair fell about her rippling and shining like a cascade of brown waters. It reached below her knee and made itself almost a garment for her. And then she did it up again nervously and quickly. Once she faltered for a minute and stood still while a tear or two splashed down on the carpet.

On went her old brown jacket; on went her old brown hat. With a whirl of skirts and with the brilliant sparkle still in her eyes, she fluttered out the door and down the stairs to the street.

Where she stopped the sign read: "Mme. Sofronie. Hair Goods of All Kinds." One flight up Della ran, and collected herself, panting. Madame, large, too white, chilly, hardly looked the "Sofronie."

"Will you buy my hair?" asked Della.

"I buy hair," said Madame, "Take yer hat off and let's have a sight at the looks of it."

Down rippled the brown cascade.

"Twenty dollars," said Madame, lifting the mass with a practiced hand.

"Give it to me quick," said Della.

Oh, and the next two hours tripped by on

rosy wings. Forget the hashed metaphor. She was ransacking the stores for Jim's present.

She found it at last. It surely had been made for him and no one else.

There was no other like it in any of the stores, and she had turned all of them inside out. It was a platinum fob chain simple and chaste in design, properly proclaiming its value by substance alone and not by meretricious ornamentation—as all good things should do. It was even worthy of The Watch. As soon as she saw it she knew that it must be Jim's. It was like him. Quietness and value—the description applied to both. Twenty-one dollars they took from her for it, and she hurried home with the 87 cents. With that chain on his watch Jim might be properly anxious about the time in any company. Grand as the watch was, he sometimes looked at it on the sly on account of the old leather strap that he used in place of a chain.

When Della reached home her intoxication gave way a little to prudence and reason. She got out her curling irons and lighted the gas and went to work repairing the ravages made by generosity added to love. Which is always a tremendous task, dear friends—a mammoth task.

Within forty minutes her head was covered with tiny, close-lying curls that made her look wonderfully like a truant schoolboy. She looked at her reflection in the mirror long, carefully, and critically.

"If Jim doesn't kill me," she said to herself, "before he takes a second look at me, he'll say I look like a Coney Island chorus girl. But what could I do—oh! what could I do with a dollar and eighty-seven cents?"

At 7 o'clock the coffee was made and the frying-pan was on the back of the stove hot and ready to cook the chops.

Jim was never late. Della doubled the fob chain in her hand and sat on the corner of the table near the door he always entered. Then she heard his step on the stair away down on the first flight, and she turned white for just a moment. She had a habit of saying little silent prayers about the simplest everyday things, and now she whispered: "Please God, make him think I'm pretty."

The door opened and Jim stepped in and closed it. He looked thin and very serious. Poor fellow, he was only twenty-two—and to be burdened with a family! He needed a new overcoat and he was without gloves.

Jim stopped inside the door, as immovable as a setter at the scent of quail. His eyes were fixed upon Della, and there was an expression in them that she could not read, and it terrified her. It was not anger, nor surprise, nor disapproval, nor horror, nor any of the sentiments that she had been prepared for. He simply stared at her fixedly with that peculiar expression on his face. . . .

Out of his trance Jim seemed quickly to wake. He enfolded his Della. For ten seconds let us regard with discreet scrutiny some inconsequential object in the other direction. Eight dollars a week or a million a year—what is the difference? A mathematician or a wit would give you the wrong answer. The magi brought valuable gifts, but that was not among them. This dark assertion will be illuminated later on.

Jim drew a package from his overcoat pocket and threw it upon the table.

"Don't make any mistake, Dell," he said, "about me. I don't think there's anything in the way of a haircut or a shave or a shampoo that could make me like my girl any less. But if you'll unwrap that package you may see why you had me going a while at first."

White fingers and nimble tore at the string and paper. And then an ecstatic scream of joy; and then, alas! a quick feminine change to hysterical tears and wails, necessitating the immediate employment of all the comforting powers of the lord of the flat.

For there lay The Combs—the set of combs, side and back, that Della had worshiped for long in a Broadway window. Beautiful combs, pure tortoise shell, with jewelled rims—just the shade to wear in the beautiful vanished hair. They were expensive combs, she knew, and her heart had simply craved and yearned over them without the least hope of possession. And now, they were hers, but the tresses that should have adorned the coveted adornments were gone.

But she hugged them to her bosom, and at length she was able to look up with dim eyes and a smile and say: "My hair grows so fast, Jim!"

And then Della leaped up like a little singed cat and cried, "Oh, oh!"

Jim had not yet seen his beautiful present. She held it out to him eagerly upon her open palm. The dull precious metal seemed to flash with a reflection of her bright and ardent spirit.

"Isn't it a dandy, Jim? I hunted all over town to find it. You'll have to look at the time a hundred times a day now. Give me your watch. I want to see how it looks on it."

Instead of obeying, Jim tumbled down on the couch and put his hands under the back of his head and smiled.

"Dell," said he, "let's put our Christmas presents away and keep 'em a while. They're too nice to use just at present. I sold the watch to get the money to buy your combs. And now suppose you put the chops on."

The magi, as you know, were wise men—wonderfully wise men—who brought gifts to the Babe in the manger. They invented the art of giving Christmas presents. Being wise, their gifts no doubt were wise ones, possibly bearing the privilege of exchange in case of duplication. And here I have lamely related to you the uneventful chronicle of two foolish children in a flat who most unwisely sacrificed for each other the greatest treasures of their house. But in a last word to the wise of these days let it be said that of all who give gifts these two were the wisest. Of all who give and receive gifts, such as they are wisest. Everywhere they are wisest. They are the magi.

—O. HENRY

19 ◆ Tell your wife how terrific she looks.

Shall I compare thee to a summer's day?

—WILLIAM SHAKESPEARE

20 ◆ Remember that the best marriage is one where your love for each other is greater than your need for each other.

Love does not consist in gazing at each other, but in looking outward together in the same direction.

—ANTOINE DE SAINT-EXUPÉRY

Apache Wedding Blessing

Now you will feel no rain, for each of you will be shelter to the other. Now you will feel no cold, for each of you will be warmth to the other. Now there is no more loneliness, for each of you will be companion to the other. Now you are two bodies, but there is only one life for both of you. Go now to your dwelling place to enter into the days of your togetherness. And may your days be good and long upon the earth.

I knew we would get married
when we started talking
about what it would be like
to grow old together.

—Joanna Dobbs

21 ◆ Marry someone you love to talk to. As you get older, his or her conversational skills will be as important as any other.

The wedlock of minds is greater than that of bodies.

—Desiderius Erasmus

22 ◆ Remember that a lasting marriage is built on commitment, not convenience.

So fall asleep, love,
loved by me.
For I know love,
I am loved by thee.

—Robert Browning

23 ◆ Don't forget that marriage is like an empty box. It remains empty unless you put in more than you take out.

The curse which lies upon marriage is that too often the individuals are joined in their weakness rather than in their strength—each asking from the other instead of finding pleasure in giving.

—SIMONE DE BEAUVOIR

24 ◆ Be kinder than necessary.

I would like to have engraved inside every wedding band, "Be kind to one another." This is the Golden Rule of marriage and the secret to making love last through the years.

—RUDOLPH RAY

Marriage Advice from 1886

Let your love be stronger than your hate or anger. Learn the wisdom of compromise, for it is better to bend a little than to break. Believe the best rather than the worst; people have a way of living up or down to your opinion of them. Remember that true friendship is the basis for any lasting relationship. The person you choose to marry is deserving of the courtesies and kindness you bestow on your friends. Please hand this down to your children and your children's children for the more things change the more they are the same.

—JANE WELLS

25 ◆ Don't discuss important matters with the television on.

Television has proved that people will look at anything but each other.

—Ann Landers

26 ◆ Understand that true love is when the other person's happiness is more important than your own.

The mistake we make is when we seek to be loved, instead of loving.

—Charlotte Yonge

27 ◆ Create and maintain a peaceful home.

A peaceful home is as sacred a place as any chapel or cathedral.

—Bill Keane

28 ◆ When you and your wife have a disagreement, regardless of who's wrong, apologize. Say, "I'm sorry I upset you. Would you forgive me?" These are healing, magical words.

Either we're pulling together or we're pulling apart. There's really no in-between.

—Kobi Yamada

29 ◆ Spend less time worrying who's right, and more time worrying what's right.

Goodnight, Beloved. This day is almost done. When the night and morning meet it will be only an unalterable memory. So let no unkind word, no careless, doubting thought, no guilty secret, no neglected duty, no wisp of jealous fog becloud its passing.

Now, as we put our arms around each other, in a sincere and affectionate token of our deep and abiding love, let us lay aside all disturbing thoughts, all misunderstandings, all unworthiness; who is to blame is not important, only how we shall set the situation right. And so, serving and being served, loving and being loved, blessing and being blessed, we shall make a happy, peaceful home, where hearts shall never drop their leaves, but where we and our children shall learn to face life joyfully, fearlessly and triumphantly, so near as God shall give us grace.

Goodnight, Beloved.

—F. Alexander Magoun

Don't Hope, Friend . . . Decide!

While waiting to pick up a friend at the airport in Portland, Oregon, I had one of those life-changing experiences that you hear other people talk about—the kind that sneaks up on you unexpectedly. This one occurred a mere two feet away from me.

Straining to locate my friend among the passengers deplaning through the jetway, I noticed a man coming toward me carrying two light bags. He stopped right next to me to greet his family.

First he motioned to his youngest son (maybe six years old) as he laid down his bags. Then they gave each other a long, loving hug. As they separated enough to look in each other's face, I heard the father say, "It's so good to see you, son. I missed you so much!" His son smiled somewhat shyly, averted his eyes, and replied softly, "Me, too, Dad!"

Then the man stood up, gazed in the eyes of his older son (maybe nine or ten) and while cupping his son's face in his hands said, "You're already quite the young man. I love you very much, Zach!" They too hugged a most loving, tender hug.

While this was happening, a baby girl (perhaps one or one-and-a-half) was squirming excitedly in her mother's arms, never once taking her little eyes off the wonderful sight of her returning father. The man said, "Hey, baby girl!" as he gently took the child from her mother. He quickly kissed her face all over and then held her close to his chest while rocking her from side to side. The little girl instantly relaxed and simply laid her head on his shoulder, motionless in pure contentment.

After several moments, he handed his daughter to his oldest son and declared, "I've saved the best for last!" and proceeded to give his wife the longest, most passionate kiss I ever remember seeing. He gazed into her eyes for several seconds and then silently mouthed, "I love you so much!"

They stared into each other's eyes, beaming big smiles at one another, while holding both hands. For an instant they reminded me of newlyweds, but I knew by the age of their kids that they couldn't possibly be. I puzzled about it for a moment, then realized how totally engrossed I was in the wonderful display of unconditional love not more than an arm's length away from me. I suddenly felt uncomfortable, as if I were invading something sacred, but was amazed to hear my own voice nervously ask, "Wow! How long have you two been married?"

"Been together fourteen years total, married twelve of those," he replied, without breaking his gaze from his lovely wife's face.

"Well then, how long have you been away?" I asked.

The man finally turned and looked at me, still beaming his joyous smile. "Two whole days!"

Two days??! I was stunned. By the intensity of the greeting, I had assumed he'd been gone for at least several weeks—if not months. I know my expression betrayed me. I said almost offhandedly, hoping to end my intrusion with some semblance of grace (and to get back to searching for my friend), "I hope my marriage is still that passionate after twelve years!"

The man suddenly stopped smiling. He looked me straight in the eye, and with a forcefulness that burned right into my soul, he told me something that left me a different person. He told me, "Don't hope, friend . . . decide."

Then he flashed me his wonderful smile again, shook my hand and said, "God bless!" With that, he and his family turned and strode away together.

I was still watching that exceptional man and his special family walk out of sight when my friend came up to me and asked, "What 'cha looking at?" Without hesitation, and with a curious sense of certainty, I replied, "My future!!"

—Michael D. Hargrove

30 ◆ When you realize you've made a mistake, take immediate steps to correct it.

If two people who love each other let a single instant wedge itself between them, it grows—it becomes a month, a year, a century; it becomes too late.

—Jean Giraudoux

31 ◆ In disagreements with your spouse, deal with the current situation. Don't bring up the past.

To be wronged is nothing unless you continue to remember it.

—Confucius

32 ◆ Don't use words carelessly. They cannot be retrieved.

It is far easier to leave angry words unspoken than to mend the heart those words have broken.

—ANONYMOUS

33 ◆ Spend some time alone.

Let there be spaces in your togetherness.

—KAHLIL GIBRAN

Where love reigns, the
impossible may be attained.

—INDIAN PROVERB

34 ◆ Never underestimate the power of forgiveness.

The difference between holding on to a hurt or releasing it with forgiveness is the difference between laying your head at night on a pillow filled with thorns or a pillow filled with rose petals.

—Loren Fischer

35 ◆ Have your wedding invitation framed and matted.

I'm always interested in how big things begin. You know how it is; you're young, you make some decisions . . . then swish, you're seventy. You've been working your profession for over fifty years and that white-haired lady by your side has eaten over 50,000 meals with you. How do such things begin?

—Thornton Wilder

36 ◆ Send your loved one flowers. Think of a reason later.

The fragrance always stays in the hand that gives the rose.

—HADA BEJAR

37 ◆ Even when angry, treat each other with respect.

There are two different times when you should keep your mouth shut: when swimming and when angry.

—UNKNOWN

38 ◆ Energize your marriage with words of appreciation.

Most of us have more to learn, no matter how long we've been around. Recently, for example, I woke up to the fact that, if I could praise something my wife had prepared for our dinner, the whole evening would take on a brighter, happier tone. Why it took me 50 years of marriage to appreciate this simple fact, I'll never know.

—John Luther

39 ◆ Toast your love each time you and your loved one are both holding wine glasses.

How much better than wine is your love.

—Song of Solomon 4:10

A woman unsatisfied must have luxuries. But a woman who truly loves a man would sleep on a board.

—D. H. LAWRENCE

40 ◆ When your wife asks if you like her new hair-style, always say yes.

That which is loved is always beautiful.

—Norwegian Proverb

41 ◆ Remember that all good marriages have this in common: courtesy, sacrifice, and forgiveness.

Love is patient, love is kind. It does not envy, it does not boast, it is not proud. It is not rude, it is not self-seeking, it is not easily angered, it keeps no record of wrongs.

—1 Corinthians 13:4–5 (NIV)

Homework

A good marriage is like a campfire: both grow cold if left unattended. "Attending" is not something you can do only when you feel like it. A campfire will die down overnight and marriage ardor will fade if neglected. Do a little something each day to keep your marriage burning bright—something like . . .

- Compliment your spouse in front of his or her best friend.
- Greet each other at the door with a kiss and a hug.
- Next Valentine's Day buy an extra bag of small heart-shaped confection candies (with short messages on them) for romantic use throughout the coming year.
- Use a favorite picture of your loved one as a special bookmark.
- Remember the nine most important words of any marriage: *I love you. You are beautiful. Please forgive me.*
- Tonight put a love note under your spouse's pillow.

Parenting

Recognition

While attending a local high school graduation ceremony recently, the role parents play in the lives of their children came into sharp focus. It was truly a defining moment, one that I shall not soon forget.

Following the principal's opening words of welcome, the students who had received scholarships spoke briefly. One common denominator united them: each expressed appreciation to his or her parents. They thanked their parents for "all the love," "all the encouragement," "for always being there," "for the great example," "for setting high standards for yourselves and me," "for being an awesome role model." Applause followed each as he or she stepped off the stage.

The last person to speak was the class valedictorian. She took the microphone in her hand, looked across the sea of faces in the packed auditorium, and then asked, "Mom and Dad, where are you?" Scanning the crowd, but not finding them, she repeated her question, "Where are you, Mom and Dad?"

Two people stood up. Their daughter, beaming, said, "Audience, I would like to introduce you to my parents. I have asked them to stand along with me because I would not be up here today had it not been for them. And now I would like everyone to give them a big round of applause because they are the ones who deserve it more than I." And applaud they did—with such vivacity that it seemed as if the noble efforts of parents everywhere were being honored.

Parenting. This most sacred duty cannot be understated. Of this I am convinced: the firm foundation of a parent's deeply rooted commitment to his or her children may also be the springboard that launches those children to new heights. The effort to teach our young all that is good and true and worthy will bear fruit in season as surely as New England cherry trees open beneath the May sunlight. The growth within our children's souls—the product of our abiding presence and tender care—will come to bloom before us as we stand looking on in appreciation, and perhaps awe.

Maybe we, too, will hear the applause someday.

1 ◆ Remember that your child's character is like good soup. Both are homemade.

If it is desirable that our children be kind, responsible, pleasant and honest, then those qualities must be taught—not hoped for.

—James Dobson

2 ◆ Don't confuse wealth with success.

No other success in life—not being President, or being wealthy, or going to college, or writing a book, or anything else—comes up to the success of the man or woman who can feel that they have done their duty and that their children and grandchildren rise up and call them blessed.

—Theodore Roosevelt

Making the decision to have
a child—it's momentous.
It is to decide forever to
have your heart go walking
around outside your body.

—ELIZABETH STONE

3 ◆ Be alert for opportunities to show praise and appreciation.

A child is fed with milk and praise.

—MARY LAMB

4 ◆ Get your priorities straight. No one ever said on his death bed, "Gee, if I'd only spent more time at the office."

It is difficult to know what counts in the world. Most of us count credits, honor, dollars. But at the bulging center of mid-life, I am beginning to see that the things that really matter take place not in the boardrooms, but in the kitchens of the world.

—GARY ALLEN SLEDGE

5 ◆ Don't worry that you can't give your kids the best of everything. Give them *your* very best.

We didn't know how poor we were; we were rich as a family.

—Florence Griffith Joyner

6 ◆ Take good care of those you love.

I keep an eye on the bottom line, but it's not an overriding obsession. To me, P and L doesn't mean "profit and loss"—it more importantly means "people and love."

—Mary Kay Ash

7 ◆ Remember that no time spent with your children is ever wasted.

The best minute you spend is the one you invest in your family.

—KEN BLANCHARD

8 ◆ Every day show your family how much you love them with your words, with your touch, and with your thoughtfulness.

Money is not required to buy one necessity of the soul.

—HENRY DAVID THOREAU

Read One Tonight

Several years ago, I decided I needed a quiet place at home where I could write in peace. Our children were grown and gone, and the downstairs playroom, the one they had once filled with raucous laughter, was more or less available. A corner was all I needed, and for the past few years, I have spent many an hour in the peaceful solitude of that corner, relatively undisturbed, doing my thing.

That didn't change much when my granddaughter Molly was born, in Virginia. When she visited, finding a quiet place to work wasn't an issue. But at the tender age of two-and-a-half, she and her family moved back to Nashville.

One Saturday morning, not long after Molly had moved to town, I was asked to baby-sit. I wanted to help, but I was in the middle of a writing project. Should I refuse? Of course not. We could go downstairs to the playroom. She could have the run of the place while I stayed in my corner and worked. I'd be there if she needed me, but otherwise, we'd just do our respective things and be perfectly happy.

She and her mother arrived at the appointed hour. Down the stairs we went. She headed straight for the toy box, and I headed straight for my own toy, my computer. Both of us immersed ourselves in the pleasure of the moment. Each of us was blissfully unaware of the other.

That utopian state didn't last very long, however. In a matter of minutes, I felt a quiet presence nearby. I looked up from my work to see that sweet child standing two feet away, waiting patiently, looking up at me with hopeful eyes.

She was holding a book.

"Read to me, Pop-Pop," she said.

I took the book. She climbed into my lap. Then, using nothing more than the words and pictures at my disposal, I carried us both into a world of imagination. When our journey was over, she jumped from my lap, ran to the shelf, picked out another book, and hurried back.

"Read to me," she said, and I did.

My mind and my heart never returned to the project I'd been working on, but even so, that was one of the nicest days I've ever had. There is a framed, handwritten sentiment on our bedroom wall. It was written by one of our daughters many years ago. She borrowed the words from another poet. She no longer remembers who wrote the original, but the sentiment was, and still is, her own. The poem ends with these lines:

> As rich as a queen I'll never be,
> but I had a mother who read to me.

—Richard Speight

9 ◆ Don't expect the best gifts to come wrapped in pretty paper.

The greatest gift I ever received was a present my dad gave me one Christmas. He handed me a note which read: Son, this year I will give you 365 hours, an hour every day after dinner. My dad not only kept his promise, but he renewed it every year after that. It's the greatest gift I ever received in my life. I am the result of his time.

—SOMEONE'S CHILD

10 ◆ Teach your children about God.

It is from God that parents receive their children, and it is to God that they should lead them.

—DIETRICH BONHOEFFER

11 ◆ **Tell your kids how terrific they are and that you trust them.**

To feel loved, to belong, to have a place and to hear one's dignity and worth often affirmed—these are to the soul what food is to the body.

—ANNE ORTLUND

12 ◆ **Don't let your family get so busy that you don't sit down to at least one meal a day together.**

When we forget the obvious, the little joys, the meals together, the birthday celebrations, the weeping together in time of pain, the wonder of a sunset or of a daffodil peeping through the snow, we become less human.

—MADELEINE L' ENGLE

13 ◆ Work hard to create in your children a good self-image. It's the most important thing you can do to ensure their success.

My mother said to me, "If you become a soldier you'll be a general; if you become a monk you'll end up as the pope." Instead I became a painter and wound up as Picasso.

—PABLO PICASSO

14 ◆ Take family vacations whether you can afford them or not. The memories will be priceless.

Somehow, year after year, dad managed to take us on vacations he couldn't afford to provide, in order to make memories we couldn't afford to be without.

—RICHARD EXLEY

15 ◆ To help your children turn out well, spend twice as much time with them and half as much money.

Children will not remember you for the material things you provided, but for the feeling that you cherished them.

—Gail Sweet

16 ◆ Read to your children. Sing to your children. Listen to your children.

Often the deepest relationships can be developed during the simplest activities.

—Gary Smalley

17 ◆ Let your children know that regardless of what happens, you'll always be there for them.

A home is a kingdom of its own in the midst of the world, a stronghold amid life's strains and struggles.

—DIETRICH BONHOEFFER

18 ◆ Apologize immediately when you lose your temper, especially to children.

Only the wise and brave man dares own he was wrong.

—BENJAMIN FRANKLIN

Children spell "love"

T—I—M—E.

—Dr. Anthony P. Witham

19 ◆ Require your children to do their share of household chores.

In the final analysis it is not what you do for your children but what you have taught them to do for themselves that will make them successful human beings.

—ANN LANDERS

20 ◆ Even if you're financially well-to-do, have your children earn and pay part of their college tuition and all their automobile insurance.

Do not handicap your children by making their lives easy.

—ROBERT A. HEINLEIN

21 ◆ Set limits on the amount and content of television your children watch.

How soon do we forget,
What elders used to know:
That children should be carefully raised,
Not left like weeds to grow.

—Art Buck

22 ◆ Never forget that being a good parent is the greatest advantage you can give your child.

All that I am I owe to my mother. I attribute all my successes in life to the moral and intellectual education I received from her.

—George Washington

23 ◆ **Never act irresponsibly in front of family members.**

Children have never been very good at listening to their elders, but they have never failed to imitate them.

—James Baldwin

24 ◆ **Judge your success by the degree that you're enjoying peace, health, and love.**

When I come home from work and see those little noses pressed against the window pane, it is *then* I know that I am a success.

—Paul Faulkner

A Tribute to Gramps

Our grandfather attended Harvard University. For his fiftieth reunion book, a form letter was sent out asking what official titles, achievements, awards, etcetera people had received and what they had accomplished since leaving Harvard. Our mother was very upset about the way the letter was written, as it implied that unless you had achieved some higher goal, you were a failure.

As my mother's letter will attest, our grandfather was a wonderful man, whose goal was to keep his family happy. He succeeded 110 percent! Our grandpa passed away eight years ago, and not one day goes by that our hearts don't ache from missing him so much.

Dear Class Secretary of 1934,

I am answering this questionnaire on behalf of my father. My father suffered a stroke about four months ago. Although he understands mostly everything, he is not able to write or speak clearly.

You ask on your questionnaire for a list of official honors and awards received, and I am at a loss to think of any official titles my father has held. However, this is not to say that he has led an uneventful or uncharitable life. If awards were to be given for "Wonderful Father," "Exceptional Grandfather" and "Devoted Friend," then surely he would have won them all. Never in my memory has there not been time for my father to be with his children, never a problem too large that Grandpa couldn't solve it. And when his friends tell me what a fine person he is, what a devoted friend, what an understanding man, I want to tell them, "I know, I know, he's my father; I've always known this." So, although these honors were not gained by a higher education or written on diplomas or awards, they are nonetheless meaningful. They were acquired by living every day to its fullest and bringing happiness to his children, grandchildren, and friends.

So, under the titles of honors on your questionnaire, the best honor of all, I suppose, is mine. I am honored to say Harold Poster is my father.

Sincerely,
Patricia Levin

The response to our mother's letter followed a few days later:

Dear Mrs. Levin:

As Secretary of the Class and Editor of the Fiftieth Report, I have the task of reviewing all of the questionnaires returned before they proceed to the printer. I say "task," but generally speaking, it is usually a pleasure. Of all those reviewed, I couldn't help but write you about the one I considered the most warm and satisfying contribution for our Fiftieth Report. I can tell you without reservation that it served to describe a person who has achieved honor and success in his life far exceeding the vast majority who have listed paragraph after paragraph of alleged honors and successes (financial, to be sure!).

My only regret is that I did not know your father in college and in the intervening years. Now I know what a truly fine man he is and a lucky person to have produced a replica in you. I do hope he is well on the road to recovery.

Many thanks for your reply!

Sincerely,
John M. Lockwood
Class of 1934 Secretary

—Dana O'Connor and Melissa Levin

I've said it a thousand times and I'll say it again: There is no job more important than that of being a good parent. None.

—Oprah Winfrey

25 ◆ Live so that when your children think of fairness, caring, and integrity, they think of you.

The first and greatest gift we can bestow on our children is to be a good example.

—Sir Charles Morell

26 ◆ Compliment even small improvements.

There is no such thing as an insignificant improvement.

—Tom Peters

27 ◆ Never use the words, "Do as I say, not as I do."

When you walk your talk, people listen.

—German Proverb

28 ◆ Drive as you wish your kids would.

There is just one way to bring up a child in the way he should go, and that is to travel that way yourself.

—Abraham Lincoln

Who you are speaks so loudly I can't hear what you're saying.

—Ralph Waldo Emerson

Catch of a Lifetime

He was eleven years old and went fishing every chance he got from the dock at his family's cabin on an island in the middle of a New Hampshire lake.

On the day before the bass season opened, he and his father were fishing early in the evening, catching sunfish and perch with worms. Then he tied a small silver lure and practiced casting. The lure struck the water and caused colored ripples in the sunset, then silver ripples as the moon rose over the lake.

When his pole doubled over, he knew something huge was on the other end. His father watched with admiration as the boy skillfully worked the fish alongside the dock.

Finally, he very gingerly lifted the exhausted fish from the water. It was the largest one he had ever seen, but it was a bass.

The boy and his father looked at the handsome fish, gills playing back and forth in the moonlight. The father lit a match and looked at his watch. It was 10 P.M.—two hours before the season opened. He looked at the fish, then at the boy.

"You'll have to put it back, son," he said.

"Dad!" cried the boy.

"There will be other fish," said his father.

"Not as big as this one," cried the boy.

He looked around the lake. No other fishermen or boats were anywhere around in the moonlight. He looked again at his father.

Even though no one had seen them, nor could anyone ever know what time he caught the fish, the boy could tell by the clarity of his father's voice that the decision was not negotiable. He slowly worked the hook out of the lip of the huge bass and lowered it into the black water.

The creature swished its powerful body and disappeared. The boy suspected that he would never again see such a great fish.

That was 34 years ago. Today, the boy is a successful architect in New York City. His father's cabin is still there on the island in the middle of the lake. He takes his own son and daughters fishing from the same dock.

And he was right. He has never again caught such a magnificent fish as the one he landed that night long ago. But he does see that same fish—again and again—every time he comes up against a question of ethics.

For, as his father taught him, ethics are simple matters of right and wrong. It is only the practice of ethics that is difficult. Do we do right when no one is looking? Do we refuse to cut corners to get the design in on time? Or refuse to trade stocks based on information that we know we aren't supposed to have?

We would if we were taught to put the fish back when we were young. For we would have learned the truth.

The decision to do right lives fresh and fragrant in our memory. It is a story we will proudly tell our friends and grandchildren. Not about how we had a chance to beat the system and took it, but about how we did the right thing and were forever strengthened.

—JAMES P. LENFESTEY

29 ◆ Become your child's best teacher and coach.

One father is more than a hundred school-masters.

—GEORGE HERBERT

30 ◆ Remember that a good example is the best sermon.

I learned more about Christianity from my mother than from all the theologians in England.

—JOHN WESLEY

31 ◆ Praise your children's efforts as well as their successes.

People are in greater need of your praise when they try and fail, than when they try and succeed.

—Bob Moawad

32 ◆ Discipline with a gentle hand.

Humans take contradiction and advice much more easily than people think, only they will not bear it when violently given, even if it is well-founded. Hearts are like flowers; they remain open to the softly falling dew, but shut up in the violent downpour of rain.

—George Matthew Adams

Standing Tall

When I was a sophomore in high school, we moved to a new town and a new high school. One of the fastest ways to make friends in that situation is to go out for a sport. In about two days you know more guys from playing ball than you could meet in three months.

Normally, I would have gone out for basketball. But I had brought home a D on my last report card because I had horsed around in the class and exhibited some very irresponsible behavior in turning in papers. My dad had a rule for the three boys in our family: if any of us got anything lower than a C, we couldn't play ball. He didn't demand that we get straight As or make the honor roll. My dad knew that the only reason any of us would get a D was that we were fooling around instead of acting in a responsible way.

Now my dad was all for me playing ball. He had been all-state in both basketball and football in high school, went to college on a basketball scholarship, and after World War II, was offered a contract to play football for the Pittsburgh Steelers. He wanted me to play. But he was more interested in developing my character than he was in developing my jump shot. My dad had some long-term goals for me that were more important than basketball.

One day I was in my physical education class, and we were playing basketball. I didn't know it but the varsity coach was in the bleachers watching the pickup game. After we went into the locker room he came up to me and asked me who I was and why I wasn't out for varsity basketball. I told him that we had just recently moved into town and that I'd come out for basketball next year. He said that he wanted me to come out this year.

I told him that my dad had a rule about getting any grade lower than a C.

The coach said, "But according to the school rules you're still eligible to play if you have just one D."

"Yes, sir, I realize that," I replied. "But you have to understand that my dad has his own eligibility rules."

"What's your phone number?" the coach asked. "I'm going to call your dad."

This coach was a big, aggressive guy. He was about six feet two inches and 220 pounds. Coach was used to getting his own way. But he hadn't met my dad. I knew before the coach ever called what my dad's answer would be.

Was my dad capable of change? Sure he was. Was he going to change because he got a call from the varsity coach? Of course not. A lot of dads would have been so flattered that they would have compromised.

That night after dinner Dad told me that the coach had called. He told me he had told the coach no. He then reminded me of the importance of being responsible in class and that he really wanted me to play basketball. But the ball was in my court (no pun intended). If I wanted to play ball it was up to me. At that point, I was very motivated to work hard in class so that I could play basketball the next season.

The next morning the coach came up to me in the locker room.

"I talked to your dad yesterday afternoon and he wouldn't budge. I explained the school eligibility rules, but he wouldn't change his mind. I don't have very much respect for your father."

I couldn't believe my ears. This coach didn't respect my father. Even I had enough sense to know my dad was doing the right thing. Sure, I wanted to play ball but I knew my dad was a man of his word and he was right in not letting me play. I couldn't believe this coach would say such a thing.

"Coach," I said, "I can tell you that I

highly respect my dad. And I also want you to know that I will never play basketball for you."

I never did. I got my grades up, but I never went out for varsity basketball. I refused to play for a man who didn't respect my dad for doing what was right. That was the end of my high school basketball career because the man coached basketball for my remaining years in high school.

Why wouldn't I play for him? Because he didn't respect my father. If he didn't have the sense to respect my dad then I sure as heck wasn't going to play for him. Come to think of it, the real reason I wouldn't join his team was that I didn't respect him. He was a compromiser and I suspected that he would do anything to win. My dad was a man of conviction and a man of character. And any coach who couldn't see that was not the kind of man I wanted to associate with. My dad was strict and unwilling to change, but he was unwilling to change because he had a long-term objective for my life that the coach didn't have.

The coach wanted to win games. My dad wanted to build a son.

—Steve Farrar

33 ◆ Give thanks before every meal.

No nation ever had a better friend than the mother who taught her children to pray.

—Anonymous

34 ◆ Spend twice as much time praising as you do criticizing.

More people are flattered into virtue than bullied out of vice.

—Robert Surtees

35 ◆ Avoid sarcasm in conversations with children.

A torn jacket is soon mended; but hard words bruise the heart of a child.

—Henry Wadsworth Longfellow

36 ◆ No matter how old you get, hug and kiss your mother whenever you greet her.

Your children are always your babies, even if they have gray hair.

—Janet Leigh

Homework

Good parenting is not easy, and it's never mistake free. But you must keep trying. Make small efforts to understand your children, to be a good example, and most of all to show them you love them. Here are a few suggestions that will help along those lines.

- Avoid using the phrase "when I was your age" when trying to make a point to your children.
- Ask your child to read to you their favorite story.
- Carry photos of your children in your wallet or purse. Don't be shy in showing them.
- When a child says he's bored, load him up and take him to the nearest museum or library.
- Place prominently on the fridge any artwork that your child brings home from school.
- Remember that sometimes the best way to clean a child's room is to just close the door.

Acknowledgments

For permission to reprint copyrighted material, grateful acknowledgment is made to the following publishers, authors, and agents. Every effort has been made to trace ownership and, when necessary, to obtain permission for each selection included.

Pages 16–21, "Is There a Santa Claus?" by William J. Lederer. Used by permission.

Pages 27–28, "A Random Act of Kindness" retold in cooperation with the staff of the Waldorf-Astoria.

Pages 49–50, "The 57¢ Difference" was originally printed in the book *From My Heart*. Copyright © 1991 by Mary Kay Cosmetics, Inc. Reprint permission granted by Mary Kay Inc. All rights reserved by Mary Kay Inc.

Pages 54–56, "No Greater Love" by Col. John W. Mansur. Reprinted with permission from the August 1987 *Reader's Digest*. Originally appeared in *The Missileer* on February 13, 1987.

Pages 61–64, "A Coincidence?" by Ed Koper. Reprinted by permission of Edward M. Koper. Copyright © 1997 by Edward M. Koper.

Pages 92–93, "Sensory Deprivation" by Deborah E. Hill. Copyright © 1999 by Deborah E. Hill. Used by permission.

Page 99, "How Much Is Enough?" from *The Song of the Bird* by Anthony de Mello. Copyright © 1982 by Anthony de Mello, S. J. Used by permission of Doubleday, a division of Random House, Inc.

Page 105, "A Flight of Geese" by Fred Lloyd Cochran. Reprinted by permission of Fred Lloyd Cochran. Copyright © 1999 by Fred Lloyd Cochran.

Page 125, from *Strengthening Your Grip* by Charles Swindoll. Copyright © 1982 by Charles Swindoll. Published by Word Publishing, Nashville, Tennessee. All rights reserved. Used by permission.

Page 132, the Optimist Creed reprinted with the approval of Optimist International, an association of civic service clubs.

Pages 179–181, "Don't Hope, Friend . . . Decide" by Michael D. Hargrove. Copyright © 1997 by Michael D. Hargrove. All rights reserved. Used with permission.

Pages 200–201, "Read One Tonight" from *Read One Tonight & Call Me in the Morning* by Richard Speight, Abingdon Press, 1998. Copyright © 1998 by Richard Speight. Used by permission.

Pages 211–213, "A Tribute to Gramps" by Dana O'Connor and Melissa Levin. Copyright © 1997 by Dana O'Connor and Melissa Levin. Used with permission.

Pages 218–220, "Catch of a Lifetime" by James P. Lenfestey. Reprinted with permission, Minneapolis *Star Tribune*.

Pages 223–226, "Standing Tall." Excerpted from *Standing Tall,* copyright © 1994 by Steve Farrar. Used by permission of Multnomah Publishers Inc.

Highlighted in Yellow, Volume II

If you recieved an instruction or piece of advice from your parents or grandparents that was especially meaningful and would like for us to share it with readers in future editions of *Highlighted in Yellow,* please write and tell us about it.

We also welcome your favorite stories. These can be original stories you have written or stories you found in a newspaper, newsletter, magazine, or even in another book.

Upcoming chapter subjects being planned at this time include: HOPE, DETERMINATION, COURAGE, SELF-DISCIPLINE, FAITH, THRIFT, CHARACTER, COURTESY, AND BIG DREAMS.

You may contact us at:

Highlighted in Yellow
P.O. Box 150155
Nashville, TN 37215

We look forward to hearing from you!

H Jackson Brown, Jr., and Rochelle Pennington

Other Books by H. Jackson Brown, Jr.

A Father's Book of Wisdom
P.S. I Love You
Life's Little Instruction Book™ (volumes I, II, and III)
Live and Learn and Pass It On (volumes I, II, and III)
Wit and Wisdom from the Peanut Butter Gang
The Little Book of Christmas Joys (with Rosemary C. Brown and Kathy Peel)
A Hero in Every Heart (with Robyn Spizman)
Life's Little Treasure Books
On Marriage and Family, On Wisdom, On Joy,
On Success, On Love, On Parenting, Of Christmas Memories,
Of Christmas Traditions, On Hope, On Friendship, On Fathers,
On Mothers, On Things That Really Matter, On Simple Pleasures
Kids' Little Treasure Books
On Happy Families
On What We've Learned . . . So Far
Life's Little Instructions from the Bible (with Rosemary C. Brown)
Life's Little Instruction Book™ for Incurable Romantics (with Robyn Spizman)
Lifes's Little Instruction Book™ from Mothers to Daughters (with Kim Shea)
A Book of Love for My Son (with Hy Brett)
A Book of Love for My Daughter (with Kim Shea and Paula Y. Flautt)